GETTING THE BEST OUT OF PEOPLE

Invest in People to Get
the Best Out of Them

FERDINARD SENYO LAWSON
Multiple Award-winning Author / Authentic Leadership Coachl
Award-winning Lifestyle and Personal Developer / Health and
wellbeing champion / Public Health Professional

GETTING THE BEST OUT OF PEOPLE

Copyright © November, 2020 by Ferdinard Senyo Lawson
All rights reserved.

ferdinardl@hotmail.com
+447869164769

All bible quotations are from:

- Amplified Bible (AMP), Copyright © 1954, 1958, 1962, 1964, 1965, 1987 by The Lockman Foundation, La Habra, CA 90631 All rights reserved.

- Holy Bible, New International Version (NIV) ® Copyright © 1973, 1978, 1984 by International Bible Society Used by permission of Zondervan Publishing House. All rights reserved.

- PC Study Bible. Copyright © 1988-2017 Bibles oft®. Inc. All rights reserved.

- The King James Version (KJV) Electronic Database. Copyright © 1988-2006, by Biblesoft, Inc. All rights reserved.

- The Message: The Bible in Contemporary Language, issued by contractual arrangement with NavPress, a division of The Navigators, U.S.A. Originally published by NavPress in English. Copyright © 2002 by Eugene H. Peterson. All rights reserved.

- The Living Bible – Copyright 1971 Tyndale House Publishers.

To my deceased grandmother, Madam Felicia Ami Ocloo, who never gave up on me but dedicated her life to introduce me to GOD. Grandma, thank you and may your soul continue to rest with God. Introducing me to Jesus Christ was the best gift you have left with me.

ACKNOWLEDGEMENTS

Success is a community project; and this piece was only realized, thanks to the contributions of several people who have played vital roles in my life. In that regard, my gratitude goes to:

- The Trinity (God, Jesus Christ, and the Holy Ghost) for the grace to write this book to inspire and transform my world.

- Bishop William Wood of Power Centre Church, Mitcham, London, United Kingdom; who believes in me and never stops to empower, encourage, motivate, and support me in my writing ministry. Man of God, I really appreciate and value you so much for all your unfailing and unwavering love and trust especially all the opportunities you give me to speak on your platforms.

- To all my mentees across the globe especially to those whom I have inspired and motivated over the years. There is more in you than you have explored. Step up and chisel the gold out of your mine.

TO MY MENTORS

1. Rev. Dr. Paul Yaw Frimpong-Manso (General Superintendent of the General Council of Assemblies of God, Ghana); words cannot express my gratitude to you for your support, kindness, prayers, and encouragement. Thank you for the seed you have sown into my life. God bless you.

2. My spiritual mentor, Pastor Charles Owusu (Deeper Christian Life Bible Church. Ghana); you are a great inspiration to me and my family both here in the United Kingdom and Ghana. God bless you.

3. To my spiritual mentor, Rev. Kingsley Amoah; you have been a strong pillar of encouragement and inspiration to me and, most importantly, my family. God bless you.

4. Pastor George Yeboah; words cannot describe my gratitude to you for your support, kindness, prayer, and encouragement.

5. Dr. Pauline Long, Dr. Ibrahim Asante and Dr. Dayo Olumo (The three lions). Meeting you has inspired and challenged me to believe in myself. You taught and gave me the injection for success, paved the way, showed me love and understanding especially when my very world gave up

on me, thinking nothing good could ever emanate from me. You helped chisel the gold out of my mine. Now the world is enjoying the light of gold in me. Thank you all.

6. My wife, Deborah, and my children (Joshua and Jessica); words cannot express how much I love you. You have inspired me to write this book. Looking at you each day gives me joy, happiness, and fulfillment. Without you, I wouldn't have discovered the gold within me. Thank you for being patient with me; for having taken yet another challenge which decreases the amount of time I spend with you. Thank you.

7. My parents (Mr. and Mrs. Lawson) and siblings; God bless you so much for the foundation of education and training you gave me during my formative years. May God continue to keep you alive to reap the fruits of your hard work. Your labor shall not be in vain.

8. My parents-in-law especially His Excellency Honorable Justice Joseph B. Akamba; you instilled in me the idea to turn my knowledge into articles. I can gratefully say that they are now in books. I want to say thank you so much for being an inspiration. God bless you.

FAILING TO SEE THE IMPORTANCE OF OTHERS IN YOUR LIFE WILL LIMIT YOU FROM ENJOYING THE BENEFITS THEY REPRESENT

TABLE OF CONTENTS

Acknowledgements v

To My Mentors vii

Preface xi

01 | Communicate Effectively With People 1

02 | Empowering People 13

03 | Providing Feedback 25

04 | The Art of Delegation (Passing On The Baton) 39

05 | Be A Mentor, Not A Manipulator 51

06 | Be Sincere And Honest With People 65

07 | Believe In Their Success 75

08 | Be A Good Planner 85

09 | Be A Disciplined Leader 97

Conclusion 106

PREFACE

The people in your life can determine your success or failure depending on how you relate with them. No one is self-made. No matter how rich and famous you are, your present state is due (in part) to the contributions of others. We all need people in our lives. From the day we are born until we exit the earth, we stand in perpetual need of human company and help. No one is useless no matter how we see them. Everyone is useful.

No matter how sophisticated life appears to be in the 21st Century, the greatest asset in life is people. Nothing can ever replace the fundamental value of people. People are agents of change and, as such, they have the ability to change the direction of your life for better or worse. Therefore, your ability to bring out the best in people is a strategic way to invest in your future.

Getting the best out of people takes more than just motivation and empowerment. Dealing with people is never an easy task, let alone bringing out the best in them. You need to be aware of people dynamics and what gets them going in order to help bring out the best in them. Apart from interpersonal skills, knowing what you really want is critical. This helps us to collaborate with others, identify their talents, skills, or gifts embedded in them and invest in them to develop and deploy those talents as a means of adding value to humanity.

Bringing out the best in people will demand our tenacity and persistence. Sometimes, the very people we try to help can be difficult, but we must not give up or be distracted. Instead, we must demonstrate passion and patience with intelligence to help bring out the best in them.

As far as health is concerned, we need people to provide us with quality care. Patients need healthcare professionals for their health needs while healthcare professionals also need patients to demonstrate their skills and expertise. The same applies to business. Business owners need customers to buy their products while customers need businessmen and women to supply them products.

Students, teachers, pastors, evangelists, prophets and apostles all need one another to function in their respective roles. Without people, nothing can be achieved in life. This is why it is very important to value the people in our lives and never take them for granted.

For example, an author who wants to publish a book needs an editor, graphic designer, typesetter, promoter, and possibly someone to help advertise the book. No one can achieve lasting success by working alone.

It takes people to make a good team. Without people, there would be nothing like teamwork. Football teams are the greatest examples of how important people are. A player can be very skillful and talented, but without the help of the rest of his teammates, he can never score a goal or become the man of the match.

People are the most valuable assets in life. Without a shadow of doubt, they hold the core of our success. The way we treat people determines how they treat us. It's common to hear people speak against others. Some complain without complimenting the efforts others made in shaping and making them into who they are.

Mentees need mentors just as mentors need mentees; leaders need followers to lead. A leader who is on the frontline without people following him or her is like a man taking a stroll by the seaside. To have a great and mega church, the pastor needs people to preach to.

People should not be classified as a number or unit but as special with unique needs. In hospitals, a patient is regarded as an individual with personal needs. This is how patient care is assessed for planning and the provision of quality care.

People are priceless. You may replace goods and services but replacing people can be a very difficult thing to do especially if they are of great value to us. You may try to replace people with machines to carry out a particular task, but I can assure you that you need people to build and operate those machines. This makes people valuable and irreplaceable.

Organizations that thrive have learnt to build around people. Failing to build around the people in your life is failing to succeed. Every forward-looking organization builds with people in mind. This is why if a leader thinks he or she has arrived and doesn't need people, he or she is bound to fail in his or her leadership.

Anyone who fails to appreciate people will surely fail in life. Without people, the world wouldn't be what it is now. People can make or break you depending on the attitude you manifest around them. Never build against people, but build with them. Doing this only creates a sense of belief, trust, loyalty, and confidence in them to build with you.

People like to be treated with respect. Nobody likes to be controlled, undermined, undervalued, abused, and taken for granted. However, if people see that they are being treated with respect, they are humble, gracious, interested, enthusiastic and respectful. Consequently, they go an extra mile to provide anything you need.

As a lifestyle coach and transformational speaker, I can boldly say that without people, success can never be achieved. People are catalysts for success. They have more to offer any organization than the organization can offer them. When people are encouraged, they can give their best to enhance the success and progress of the team they are in.

You shouldn't expect productivity if you have not empowered the people in your team

A leader who empowers people will always see productivity and success in whatever he or she does. The sad thing these days is that most people have lost interest in others simply because they have come to value material wealth over people; hence the killing of people for fame and wealth.

Regardless of how we want to be rich and famous, we must not prioritize anything above the lives of the people God has put in our space. It is very important that we learn to value people above money, structures, systems, and other institutional machinery.

Nothing should take the place of people. We must not devalue people, but love and cherish them whether in-person or online. People are people and nothing can replace them and so we ought to value and treat them with respect and dignity. People (rich or poor, leader or follower, cleaner or manager, pastor or church member) may be victims of circumstances but it does not mean they should be treated like objects.

One good thing about people is that they bring variety into our lives. They hail from different religions and cultures; they have different interests and personalities, and contribute to community-building with their diversity and uniqueness. It is therefore my earnest prayer and wish that as a society, we will begin to appreciate, embrace, and celebrate the people we are fortunate to meet on a daily basis.

We must learn to respect and treat people as fellow human beings but not as objects or inanimate entities. Leaders (especially church leaders) should do more to invest in the growth of their members to ensure their growth spiritually, economically, and socially. Remember that when we invest in people, we are investing in the development of our world.

Nonetheless, people are different due to various reasons. Some of these reasons spring from a person's background (upbringing), culture, beliefs, and personal values. As such, these contribute to how they perceive and process things from different perspectives.

Moreover, trying to help people with their gifts and talents will take diverse forms. This is why we need to change some of the methods we employ in helping people and start acting professionally with people to bring out the best in them.

No one succeeds in isolation. This is why we all need somebody to help us bring out the best in us.

I have no doubt that history has a lot to teach us about people who were overlooked by those who had the power and opportunity to help them bring out the best in them but failed them, by suppressing those talents, gifts, and skills.

Irrespective of who you are or what you do, never undermine the power you have to bring out the best in people. Many people have lots of great ideas and inventive strategies who are waiting and looking for you and me to lend them a helping hand.

God never wastes resources. So, amazingly, He has deposited special talents in everyone on this planet. Therefore, it is our collective responsibility to identify people with such special talents such as football, boxing, running, tennis, dancing, singing, etc. and invest our resources to bring out the best in them.

As a people, we are like children who need patience, time, and understanding to grow and develop character and other inbuilt talents. Therefore, bringing out the best in others will require us motivating them to develop a positive mindset; give them the needed platforms through which they can find new ways of looking at their abilities, learn from their mistakes, and boldly express their essence.

As you read this book, may you begin to explore around to identify those who need your support in order to develop their innovative ideas to provide the human capacity we all need to live.

Bringing out the best in people will help you get on well with people as well as enhance your personal and professional life.

Above all, to succeed and win with people, you must respect, value, and treat people as individuals and not as groups in order for them to give you their best in whatever they do.

01

COMMUNICATE EFFECTIVELY WITH PEOPLE

"Everybody has the need to be listened to and be fully understood"

To get the best out of people, you need to develop the skill of communicating effectively with the people you want to help. Effective communication is one of the best ways to bring out good qualities in others.

It takes two people to have an effective and productive conversation at any level. This implies that, to get the best in people, you need to work on your communication skills.

Communicating effectively with people allows them to be open to you. It helps them to express their needs, thoughts, and ideas clearly without fear. Communication promotes value and understanding among people.

Under no circumstance should others feel less valuable in a relationship. Two people cannot walk together except they agree, and the only thing that makes that possible is effective communication.

People should be able to feel free to talk about things without feeling undermined, disregarded or disrespected especially as it relates to sensitive issues.

It has been observed that one of the main reasons most people don't get the best in others is that they fail to encourage others to express their thoughts and ideas freely as they should; hence, limiting the chances of developing and benefiting from the people in their life.

Granted, people are different with different backgrounds, values, and outlook which creates different comfort zones for them. So, they see talking about issues as a big challenge.

EFFECTIVE COMMUNICATION IS ONE OF THE VITAL KEYS TO UNLOCKING THE TREASURES IN PEOPLE

When we fail to communicate clearly with others, it creates misunderstanding, distancing, indifference, competition, and sometimes aggression. This is occasioned by the fact that we don't talk about the things that matter. The tendency is for people to bottle things up and reach a boiling point; inevitably, the predictable outcome is conflict.

Communicating our desires and expectations clearly to people is key to building healthy and intimate relationships. It pays to state exactly what we want from them, and help them to align themselves with what we want from them.

Failing to communicate effectively with people as it relates to what is expected of them can lead to people feeling confused, unmotivated, and disengaged. It is very important that we don't overstretch our expectations pertaining to those we are attached to.

Communicating your plans, ideas, and vision to your subordinates makes them work at their best because they have come to understand clearly the high standard you have set for them to have things done effectively.

Effective communication with people prevents ambiguity when it comes to the very things we want and expect from them.

Good communication entails letting people know what we want, making things clearer and ensuring that they know exactly what to do if they have queries or burning questions.

People become more committed, dedicated, and motivated to complete what is demanded of them once they can understand and relate to what is expected of them.

People mostly get down doing what is expected of them when they are closely inspected or supervised.

To get the best out of people, it is vital to be honest and sincere in the way we communicate and convey relevant information to them.

While making reference to His followers, Jesus once declared, "My sheep know my voice." People love to associate with others who are honest and real. As such, it is important that you remain consistent in your identity.

Cultivating effective communication skills helps us to listen and encourage others to contribute their quota. This requires remaining silent and patient with others when they are talking, encouraging them to offer ideas and solutions before we give our final word. When we discipline ourselves to listen more than we talk, those who have secured our listening ears become eager to express their thoughts and ideas as our patient spirit sends the message that they are valued and appreciated.

Our ability to listen to others enables us to embrace their knowledge and value their perspective about things, fostering trust, respect, and transparency.

We need to become more patient with the people we want to help and develop tolerance; giving them enough room to express themselves without feeling undermined or devalued.

Undoubtedly, one of the most important aspects of getting the best out of people is our ability to listen to them. Therefore, it follows that failing to develop this skill is failing to get the best out of them.

Sadly, many of us have failed or are failing in this area; hence, limiting or preventing ourselves from getting the best in people, making a shipwreck of their destinies and potentials.

It is very important that we pay attention to our listening skills. We must never come to the point where we become highhanded in our dealings with others. Everyone has the seed of listening and it is vital that we cultivate that seed in order to become proactive and effective.

If you desire to be great and influential in helping others bring out the best in them, you must learn to listen more and speak less.

The only way you can even learn more effectively and benefit from others is by learning to listen more. We should never hijack a conversation because of the position we hold.

We must also learn to wait and listen to what others have to say. Wisdom is the right application of knowledge which only comes to us when we learn to listen to the information being shared by others.

It is very important that we allow others to share their views especially when it comes to the progress of the organization, team, ministry, church, school, etc.

We should not be in a hurry to speak when others are speaking to us. Rather, we should learn to hold our tongue and pay attention to what is being said to us.

Listening to people creates the platform for us to actually view the world from others' perspectives.

We therefore understand and appreciate others more when we learn to listen to them, thereby creating an environment of assurance and confidentiality. This enhances our relationship with them.

Without listening to others, we can't bring out the best in them. As mentioned earlier, no matter how knowledgeable we may think we are, if we don't have the right attitude to listen to the people we want to help or develop, we will be limited in shaping them and bringing out the best in them.

Indeed, not everyone is a good listener. Some find it very challenging especially when they are in leadership positions. Surprisingly, such individuals always have problems influencing others simply because they don't connect well with people. Listening to others helps us connect, understand, and relate appropriately with people.

Interestingly, no one would like to associate himself or herself with an individual who doesn't like to listen or wait for his turn to speak. Many are too busy speaking over others in meetings just to show that they are knowledgeable than others, but will fail to influence and make positive impact on them because they don't understand the power of listening in communication.

How can you learn and make impact on others when you are the only one doing the talking? You can never become a person of influence that way.

Patiently listening to others provides us the right information required to enable us take action in the right direction. A good listener pays attention to the thoughts, feelings, and conducts of the people he or she is supporting and developing.

To get the best out of people and work smoothly with them in the right environment, it is important we encourage mutual communication between us and the people in our lives.

People who are listened to at any level, position or environment and are given the platform to communicate effectively become courageous, innovative and disciplined in their approach to life.

A common mistake most people make is that they don't offer honest feedback. They do not give the opportunity to people to present their own comments and concerns regarding what matters to personal development and growth.

EFFECTIVE COMMUNICATION IS THE FOUNDATION FOR PEOPLE DEVELOPMENT AND GROWTH

When we allow others to communicate their needs, concerns, and issues affecting them and limiting their growth, we motivate them to share their burdens.

When it comes to team building, it is very important to promote and encourage effective communication among all team members helping them to operate and work together in achieving positive outcomes.

Effective communication helps us to create opportunities for people to share knowledge acquired with others without fear.

Although it is possible that some people find it difficult to talk about some vital personal experiences (especially subjects like their childhood relationships and how it ended up badly, or their past life) due to painful memories or hurts, it is my heart's desire that after reading this book, we will be able to unlearn, relearn, and learn how to talk more effectively with others regardless of our past experiences.

This will help us to develop the genuine desire to learn and embrace others no matter their backgrounds.

Everything about getting the best out of people is built around communication. It plays a vital role in developing others into their best.

Communication is everything in life. Life cannot be interesting or fun without communication. In fact, without effective communication, life is meaningless.

Communication helps us give and receive relevant information from the people we want to help.

Just as oxygen is to the body, communication is also vital in determining the quality of our relationships; be they family or business.

Communication is the backbone of every fruitful and productive relationship. Without communication, nothing substantial can be achieved. Through communication, we express our ideas and feelings, and it helps us to understand the emotions and thoughts of others.

When communication goes wrong, people develop the wrong feelings towards one another and this may lead to friction.

Communication is a vital aspect (much like the heart) of human relationships that allows free flow of ideas, thoughts, dreams, and feelings.

The human heart is responsible for the flow of blood to the whole body. Therefore, when the heart fails, the body dies because there wouldn't be blood flow (oxygen) to parts of the body. We can thus conclude that communication is the lifeblood (heart) of every relationship. This means that when communication fails, everything dies.

Communication can be seen as manure or fertilizer, enhancing and providing nutrients to people development. Therefore, people express their thoughts and ideas comfortably around us when we allow them the liberty to do so. This helps them to discover what they want without feeling that they are being controlled.

Giving others the chance to talk about things that bother them helps to bring about transparency and creates the platform on which issues are tackled in love. This has the potential to remove any form of doubt and insecurity, loss of hope, and emotional breakdown which sometimes affects and destroys many people.

OPENNESS IS ONE OF THE BENEFITS OF EFFECTIVE COMMUNICATION IN GETTING THE BEST OUT OF OTHERS

If you ever wanted to get the best out of people, then you must learn to give them the opportunity to talk and express themselves freely and create the right environment where you can both share ideas and feelings together.

To get the best out of others, we should be able to make time for them to talk freely without being interrupted or disturbed.

When we give people the chance to talk to us uninterrupted, they feel very important, significant, relevant and valued.

Whether we are working with people in a ministry, family, institution, business, school, team or an organization, it is necessary to create room for effective communication between the people we lead and want to get the best out of.

We can easily bring out the best in others within the shortest possible time by becoming good listeners than we can in 10 years trying to impress and get them to love or understand us. Ordinary people hijack communication from others, but extraordinary individuals empower others to talk while they listen.

There is no way we can impact the lives of others and help bring out the best in them if we are not willing to take a backseat, share platforms, and empower them. We must be willing to redirect our attention on the people we lead or want to help so as to learn how to empower and motivate them to become their best. People really associate well with those they feel very comfortable talking with who are ready and prepared to listen to them.

YOU CAN ONLY HELP THE PERSON YOU LISTEN TO, NOT THE ONE YOU IGNORE

You are not in leadership to be popular, but to make impact on your followers. The only way to achieve this to pay attention and attend to the needs of your followers.

You will never know how much people love you until you give them the chance to talk and express it to you. I have always said that people are our assets in life. They can make us great or break us into pieces beyond repair and recognition.

It is very dangerous to put yourself in a place where you make others feel and think you know it all. No one wants to help anyone who thinks he or she knows it all. In fact, no one is a sole custodian of wisdom. So, if you really want to bring out the best in others, then you must be willing to hand over the microphone to others to share their thoughts, ideas, and knowledge with you.

As we grow and become more influential in society, under no circumstance should we lose the virtue of listening to others who have relevant information and ideas to share with us.

You cannot develop deaf ears around people and expect them to share ideas with you. Whenever you develop deaf ears deliberately around the people in your life, you close your mind from receiving knowledge for your next level.

When we learn to listen, we learn to build others up with what we know. Listening attentively to people enables them to share great and innovative ideas with us because they will go out of their way to share their secrets and future plans with us. If we show people how much we care by listening to them, we will be amazed by how much they tell us.

Begin to create room and make time just to listen to the people in your life. It will be very difficult in the beginning but with determination and willingness, you will do it. Spend at least one to two hours listening to your family, team, colleagues, members, mentees, children, partners, etc. without interrupting them. Pay them the price of undivided attention and see how much you will learn from them. Don't deny yourself from how much people have to tell you.

A DEAF EAR BEGETS A MIND THAT IS CLOSED TO IDEAS AND INNOVATIONS

02

EMPOWERING PEOPLE

Empowering others transforms them into great men and women. It takes a lot of empowerment to chisel out the best in people. No one is worth less if we know how to empower them, and no one remains ordinary for life if we cultivate the habit of empowering them.

It is our empowerment of others that turns them from trash into treasure. People are like clay in the potter's hands. No matter how they look, with empowerment, they can be molded into vessels unto honor and treasured by others.

The ability to empower others is one of the keys to greatness. There is no point living or being surrounded by people you cannot empower to grow and develop. People are seeds and the only way to help them grow is to nurture, invest and support them through empowerment. Empowerment is the fertilizer for personal development and greater productivity. People get better at what they do in business, family, education etc. when they are empowered.

It doesn't really matter to others how much you earn or have achieved in life if that does not translate to adding value to their lives. People are not moved by how much we impress them but by how much we impact and influence them to grow.

People grow into significance when we empower them. We are able to have positive influence on the people we inspire, motivate and empower, making them to reach their potentials and maximize their destiny. This is why empowering people is crucial to the fulfillment of their dreams.

Unless we are ready to invest our time, resources and knowledge in others, we wouldn't be able to impact them and usher them into their destiny. It is absolutely possible for one to empower others unknowingly. Life is such that our lives impact on many people without our knowledge.

For example; leading, mentoring or teaching your children some social skills aside school lessons is a form of empowerment. Allowing your teenage child to go to school, get on the public transport, and visit family and friends on his or her own is empowering. It also teaches him/her to be independent to a certain degree.

We change lives for good when we empower others. We motivate and inspire them to grow, mature, develop and nurture their talents by empowering them to use their talents to add value to their world. This means that when we empower an individual, we end up transforming a generation.

You lose nothing by empowering others to step up into their calling and purpose. You increase your level of influence and impact by empowering people.

As you go about with the business of adding value to people, you must also bear in mind that you are not called to everyone, but some people. It is your duty to identify those who really need you to empower them. You can't go standing in the middle of the road trying to empower just anyone.

You can't save the whole world. Don't even think about it. It is said that you can take a horse to the river bank, but you cannot force it to drink. Inasmuch as you would like to encourage, inspire, and motivate others to pursue their purpose in life, you should know that you can't succeed in your mission if they are not ready for what you have to offer.

You can be interested in someone's dream and aspiration but when they don't give you the authority into their life, you cannot go knocking at their doors to force down your empowerment on them. You empower whom you have power and authority over.

You can only empower others when they see the need for it. Trying hard to empower someone who is not ready will be like trying to pull out a bone stuck in between your teeth. You are bound to succeed in your endeavor when the beneficiary sees the value and the importance of what you have to offer and subscribes to it. Such a person embraces every effort you take to empower him knowing that the only way to get better in life is through capacity enhancement.

Getting the best out of people will require tons and tons of effort. This creates an environment for learning, development, and growth. People are ready and willing to share personal information (no matter how sensitive) with you when they are empowered. The feedback you provide helps them weigh options before taking critical decisions.

Team members are more inspired to achieve more and become more productive when they are empowered.

People who are willing to be empowered will be ready to avail themselves for training, mentorship and correction as that is the only way to identify pitfalls, mistakes and accept the process involved in becoming the best they can be.

Empowering people is a form of education. Education is the key that opens the window of opportunity to people. It is the foundation on which we develop and grow.

Empowering others means you actually know that people will always be people. They will make mistakes along the way. Therefore, empowering them is your way of lifting them up when they fall, educating and showing them the way so they can correct their mistakes and learn a better way to do things differently when they are faced with similar situations in the future.

As we all can appreciate, nobody is perfect. No matter how we see ourselves or what we have achieved, there will always be the need for personal development. This is why it is crucial to empower others if we are to get out the best in them. Transformation comes from sharing relevant information with the right people.

This means that empowering our team, groups or company with the right information is a way of equipping them to know how things are done. It becomes a tool in their hands to reshape and rebuild their future as it motivates and makes them feel accomplished and empowered when they are able to complete tasks independently.

Anyone who desires to get the best in others must make provision for and invest in the future of the people around them, creating platforms for the maximization of potentials. It is the duty of every leader to empower their followers or protégés to become all that they are designed for.

Leaders are meant to be pathfinders, pacesetters, and trailblazers to their followers. This means that every leader must be able to identify the needs of their protégés and learn to interact with them, empower and chisel the best out of them in order for them to become great in their area of calling.

This can only be possible when the leader makes efforts to create room for ongoing discussion of the opportunities, needs, obstacles, tasks, projects and prospects that matter to the people who are being led.

Effective and productive leaders spend quality time with their protégés to empower them into the next phase of their personal life as well as the development of their organization. Empowerment provides positive energy to every protégé or follower to undertake responsibility and operate maximally beyond limitation.

Empowering people creates room for the development of skills, ignite positive thinking, and rejuvenate winning power in people to create success. Empowerment goes a long way to enhance self-image and belief (confidence and courage) to perform a task. Many people know what to do in life but do not know how to step out of their shell of shyness and laziness to get the job done.

The leader is one who then empowers them to step out to achieve those dreams and aspirations by motivating or empowering them to do what needs to be done. This boosts their morale and desire to rise above limitation or fear that had held them from pursuing their purpose in life. An effective and productive leader is willing to take protégés along in the journey of success.

It is therefore paramount that both leaders and protégés take responsibility to avail themselves of opportunities to be empowered to achieve greater things in life.

Empowerment is a responsibility every forward-thinking leader must cultivate to see productivity in the people they lead.

For us to lead and get the best out of others, we must give people the opportunity to express and take full responsibility for what they believe and have skills to execute or deploy the knowledge they have acquired to add value to society. This will ultimately boost their confidence and help them to contribute to their personal development.

As a lifestyle coach and public health professional, I have observed that empowerment unto self-actualization as a model helps to promote self-motivation and development of one's ability to take full control of his or her own health, ensuring that he or she follows the guidelines for maintaining a healthy life.

Empowering others with the right information enhances their sense of self-esteem, personal identity, and self-worth. This enables them to make positive decisions regarding their health; knowing that, no one can live a healthy life for them but themselves.

When people are empowered, they are inspired to take necessary and required steps to develop themselves.

Empowering others encourages them to reflect and change their views on success, personal self-image and how they view the world. It instills in them the idea that they are the CEO of their lives and that all things are possible to the man/woman who believes people who are empowered or encouraged are able to build some level of confidence in themselves to pursue their dreams. They are able to chase their aspirations regardless of the challenges they face to become their best because they accept and appreciate their own worth.

When people are empowered, they are able to evaluate their own life, vision, and dreams as well as take full control of their emotional state (EMOTIONAL INTELLIGENCE) to overcome fear, failure, and whatever else that has limited or prevented them from bringing out the best in them.

Sadly, many people are living beneath their full potentials. Some have given up on their dreams, aspirations and goals simply because they feel discouraged and disappointed, given that someone let them down. Some are trying to live other people's lives and dreams and have buried their own essence. Getting the best out of people will require our investment in them to achieve.

Encouragement plays a vital role even in child development. Like children, people do well when they feel empowered and motivated instead of them being undermined, undervalued and constantly criticized. They strive to live out the inspiration injected into them. This is why it is paramount that we encourage and empower others more than we castigate and rebuke them.

We must always try to find something to congratulate and reward in people. This sends a positive message and motivates them to keep doing their best to achieve success in life.

Come what may, people need to be encouraged to step up in the pursuit of their goals and dreams with the little effort to overcome their limitations to succeed in life.

Without empowering people to pursue their dreams and aspirations, life can be very hard to live and ultimately, success will be farfetched for some as they will find it challenging to focus.

Take the case of a student who lacks motivation and therefore finds it difficult to focus on his or her studies even when the day of examination draws near. Such a student will not be happy to discipline himself to prepare and plan for anything relating to examination. This is why capacity building is critical in helping people stay focused on their dreams. So, for us to help bring the best out of others, we have to inspire them to reach their goals, aspirations, dreams, and satisfaction in life. We have to empower them to see beyond their failures, disappointment, and discouragement.

Most often, individuals who lack motivation and boldness to embrace success are happy staying in their comfort zones. They just don't like to be challenged to step out of their comfort zones because they are afraid of failure and scared to disappoint others.

This is why personally, I like to empower and encourage my children to step out to do what they have to do especially if it is not going to put their life or those of others at risk. In fact, life is full of risks, but we must empower people and allow them to take calculated risks to succeed in life.

For example, if they are thinking of becoming an author, setting up a business or losing weight, they just have to start with baby steps. For a prospective author, the journey can begin with a page a day; for someone who is business-inclined, adopting a good savings plan on their current job as a means to step out on their own to start a business subsequently works. You can progressively achieve your dream of losing weight by going to the gym for workouts once a week.

WITHOUT EMPOWERMENT, SUCCESS IS UNACHIEVABLE

While empowering others to get the best out of them, it is also mandatory that we make them understand that one can be successful in life, but without happiness, success will be meaningless.

No one likes to associate with someone who let them down, undermined and devalued; everyone enjoys the company of those who see the scars on others and yet still empower them to see the star in themselves.

As I said earlier, empowerment is one's ability to move others from inspiration to aspiration. Meaning, we must not just limit our empowerment to inspiration but encourage others to see further from where they are now so that they can get to pursue the vision ahead of them to attain.

People love the company of leaders, ministers or others who empower them to develop themselves into their dreams, and pushing them to have hope even in their hopeless situations.

This is why this book is written to help bring out the best in you for you to impact your world positively.

INVESTING IN PEOPLE CREATES THE AVENUE FOR THEM TO INVEST IN YOU GREATLY

Successful people always look for opportunities to pour themselves into others. They are never scared or insecure about the people they empower. Such individuals understand that, for them to continue to make positive impact and leave a legacy for others to emulate, they have to invest in others by motivating and empowering them to discover themselves, develop their gifts and stepping into their place and deploying their talents.

We must always value others and enjoy the benefits of being around them just as they also feel valued around us. Influential leaders don't build their kingdom at the expense of others. They see the need to invest in others alongside pushing their dream. Invest in people and they will also invest in you.

Effective and influential leaders discover, develop, and deploy people into their marketplace ministry. They don't abuse, use, or undermine people. Great and influential leaders are people developers. They are always looking for opportunities to develop others.

However, selfish leaders are always looking for avenues to exploit, use and abuse other people's time, resources, gifts and efforts to enhance or promote themselves. They never invest in others yet, want others to invest in them.

To get the best out of people, we must show interest in their interests. When we fail to show interest in the things others are passionate about, they will also not show interest in the things you are passionate about as a leader. Sow interest, and you will reap interest from others.

When we honestly and genuinely care more for the people in our lives more than what they can offer and give us as leaders, they go out of their way to build and support our ministries, churches, and organisations without fail.

Genuine love and care take away fear and doubts from the mind of the people we lead. People don't really care how much we shout and preach Jesus Christ to them, but how we make them feel with the love of Jesus Christ in you.

Treat people with respect and honour. Never take anyone for granted; you do that at your own peril. Life has a way of turning people's life around. Don't be fooled by people's present situations or conditions. You just don't know what their tomorrow brings. There is a turning-around and timing for everyone. So, be kind and sensitive in your approach to the people in your life.

It takes lots of commitment, knowledge, education, and skills to empower others. It is my wish and prayer that you identify the area in which you need to improve so as to empower the people in your life. Be empowered.

03

PROVIDING FEEDBACK

Compliment is the key that unlocks the best in people. Too many people have their talents locked up in them because those they look up to for motivation and mentorship have failed to recognize the need to compliment their efforts. Rather, they are only ready to criticize and blame them for every little mistake they make. Until we learn to compliment others, they cannot trust us to help them become their best.

If we create an atmosphere of compliment and encouragement, people will begin to trust us to help them reach their goals in life. Every little bit of compliment has the potential to motivate and build confidence in people for their next level in life.

Just as a compliment enables others to follow you, withholding it from them will discourage and send them the opposite way.

Adults, like children, get better or interested in the things they do best with genuine compliments. Giving someone a compliment is like injecting fresh blood into their system.

A genuine compliment acts like a booster, creating positive vibes and energy for one to become successful or take the right steps to achieve their goals.

If we want to get the best out of others, we will have to express how we feel about them in terms of what they are doing as it helps to boost their self-confidence and nourishes their self-belief in knowing that they are appreciated and valued.

Most often, people have low self-esteem, lack a sense of identity, and lack the boldness to step up to achieve their dreams. Complimenting them supplies the lubricant to stimulate that inner strength for them to know that, if they carry on doing their best, they will continually be appreciated.

Giving compliments creates a virtuous circle. When we compliment others, it creates the room for diligence and hunger for excellence. Telling or showing your impression towards someone's success in a driving test, for instance, will go a long way to motivate such an individual to cultivate the habit of safe driving.

As I mentioned earlier, no one likes to hang around a miserable person who never appreciates or compliments people when they have done something good. On the other hand, some people will make every effort to be with the person who gives honest compliments.

In fact, giving compliment is an aspect of effective leadership. It inspires and generates positive vibes in others, helping them become agents of positive change. People never forget how you made them feel around you as a leader, but will easily forget the gifts you gave them. This is why complimenting is very crucial in getting the best out of others. No matter the material things you give others, they will only remember how you actually made them feel regarding their failures, disappointment and discouragement.

Complimenting is an attitude we ought to develop in response to the good we see in others. This is why I see a compliment as a seed. It grows and feeds everyone. Most often, we reap what we sow in others. When we sow kindness and respect, others also shower us with kindness and respect. Nothing happens by chance but by cautious decision-making.

Just as the late Lucky Dube said, *"If you live in a glass house, you don't throw stones and if you want to be respected, then you must also learn to sow the same into others instead of cursing and being rude and arrogant to them."* The Bible also makes it clear that, whatever a man sows, that is what he will reap (Galatians 6:7). This implies that, whatever we do or invest in others will surely come back to us many times over.

As a lifestyle coach and transformational speaker, I have keenly observed that anytime I go out of my way to compliment my clients on a specific achievement, I get very happy inwardly and desire to go out to do more.

When we compliment others, it shows that we love and value them. They feel very enthusiastic about the things they do and develop the drive to do better when an opportunity presents itself in the future.

To bring out the best in others, you must begin by appreciating and complimenting the little things they do for you. You must compliment people not only for their achievements or success, but also for their tenacity in character, actions, and their choices in making the best in life.

In most relationships where both partners compliment each other as against condemning and criticizing, the result is intimacy. The level of self-esteem and trust rises in such settings. Compliments break barriers and remove unnecessary fuming from relationships. This is why it is mandatory that married couples focus on the good in each other instead of the negative. Focusing on the negative erodes and destroys the family union.

Also, in classroom settings, complimenting students inspires, motivates, and influences good behavior even amongst the most notorious and difficult students. When we give sincere compliments to students, it creates a sense of positivity in them and encourages them to look forward for a better day in school. This fires them up to pay more attention to detail and give them more incentive to do better and try harder.

A true compliment sends the message that we appreciate, cherish and value those we are commending for who they are and for what they do.

> *"People do better work when they're reminded of their track record of excellence, so it pays to give praise where it's due."*

Any employer who wants to see or get the best out of his or her team members must cultivate a culture of compliments amongst the team members as it injects worth and value in the team.

When managers or bosses give genuine and sincere compliments to their team members, it motivates and empowers them to believe in themselves and inspires them to up their game by increasing persistence in productivity and performance.

Nevertheless, complimenting doesn't mean one should tolerate laziness and a mediocre lifestyle in and around workplaces.

However, a lack of it can hinder the people in our lives from living their full potential, becoming productive in life and developing positive self-worth.

Self-worth emanates in part from compliments. Complimenting people has the ability to affect an individual's education, employment, relationship, and more.

If we want to help bring out the best in others, improve their quality of life and to set them on the road of success, then we need to compliment them accordingly.

Complimenting others makes them feel useful and good about themselves, knowing that you are supporting them into success.

Sometimes, getting the best out of others will demand that we be frank and honest with them; pointing out what is lacking in them and how they can make up for it. So, if a team member keeps punching below their weight, it becomes necessary for them to be notified about their behavior and attitude towards work so they don't infect other team members with such unproductive behavior.

Getting the best out of others means that you are very vigilant in observing their character and attitude in order to draw their attention to what they may be taking for granted. However, never criticize the person openly or publicly, but in the secret or on a one-on-one basis. That way, the person wouldn't feel undermined and devalued in front of the rest of the team.

Under no circumstance should you blame people in the open. Blaming others openly doesn't help them grow; it shuts them down and deflates any desire of them becoming their best.

Never be quick to judge or blame those you want to help grow or develop. Your ability to give them room to express themselves will give you enough room to understand the full story behind their flaws.

Just as we expect others to be patient with us when we make mistakes, we must be slow to point accusing fingers at others when they go wrong. You don't solve problems or bring the best out of others by blaming them.

Farmers don't blame the quality and quantity of their harvest on the seed; they take responsibility to assess what they did wrong to generate the level of crops they have harvested in order to make certain decisions that will lead to a bumper harvest during the next season.

LEADERSHIP ISN'T ABOUT BLAMING OTHERS; IT'S ABOUT BUILDING THEM UP FOR THE FUTURE

In leadership, you get the best from others by inspiring and motivating them rather than blaming them.

Real leaders don't take credit for success, but always claim responsibility for failure. It is very interesting how parents train their children to take responsibility for their actions, yet parents fail at their game when it comes to leadership. Parents tend to look for others to blame in order to save their heads.

When there is a failure on our part as leaders to take responsibility for our own actions and that of those we lead, it shows that we are not leaders but followers. It is important to note that we need to learn to accept our responsibility and that of others, so that we can do everything possible to help develop and bring the best out of them.

Leaders who constantly blame their team will never bring the best out of them. Blaming others will build walls that will prevent us from seeing the need to improve, develop, and empower them.

People are able to achieve their best when we make them feel loved, respected and valued. This can only be possible if we compliment them and help them cultivate a sense of belonging.

Everybody wants to be valued and respected. It is something we cannot live without. Many people, especially young adults, are not able to connect well with the older generation; therefore, they seem to be detached from the reality of life.

Majority of these young people may be feeling isolated and excluded from society. Some may seek to associate themselves with the wrong people just to boost their self-worth or identity.

In view of this, they lose their sense of belonging; of being loved and valued and this can potentially push them into delinquency.

This is why it is very important that coaches, mentors, teachers, parents and youth workers relate with young people to understand their needs (be they emotional, educational, sexual, health, etc.) and devise means to meet them at their point of need.

We should be able to give compliment to the people in our lives more than we castigate and complain about their mistakes.

A man who is afraid to fail will fail at trying. The only way to overcome failure and become a person of influence and significance is by learning from your mistakes.

Mistakes are part of human development. No one gets better in life without making mistakes. You are not the first or the last to make mistakes in life. This means that many people have made and still make serious mistakes in their life's journey. The issue is not the mistakes but one's attitude and perspective relating to mistakes.

Success is not the air one breathes. It is in the things we do and pursue regardless of the fears and challenges of failure. I have always said that, you can never become what you are afraid of. This implies that when you are afraid to make a mistake as you pursue success, you will find it difficult to attain it. There are many hurdles and challenges in life. However, our ability to rise above them gets us into the flight of success. Making mistake is not failure.

On the contrary, mistakes make us grow and develop into what we had always wanted for ourselves if we are wise enough to learn from them. Great and successful men and women have made serious and devastating mistakes in life and have used the lessons learnt to rebuild their personal life and success.

We mostly think that successful people do not make mistakes, but that is false. Most people erroneously think that making mistakes means you are a failure.

What they don't know is that, for one to have a successful story in whatever they do, they must have room for mistakes. What you do not prepare for will take you by surprise. We must learn to create room or have an open mind about mistakes. This prevents us from going down with depression when failure hits us like a tornado or tsunami.

Many people live their lives without preparing for mistakes. They therefore get deflated and get into shock mode when they make a mistake. The question is: You made a mistake, so what? To become successful in the pursuit of your dreams, goals and aspirations, you should know that you will make mistakes. Therefore, bear in mind that no one is perfect and therefore, making mistakes is another way of learning and developing into something greater than the mistake.

However, you cannot learn from your mistakes when you try to deny them. Denying your mistakes only makes you a victim of failure. This is why it is very paramount that we teach people to learn to accept their mistakes and open up for correction. Failure to do this pushes them into depths of disappointment and heartaches.

Failing to accept that you have made a mistake will also prevent others from giving you the right and needful help to make you wiser. You must be ready to admit your mistakes all the time without feeling shy or ashamed about them. This is how you get help and redirection.

No wise driver will continue to drive on the fastest road knowing very well that he or she has made the wrong turn. Life is a journey and mistakes are like the junctions of life. You never stop going or travelling on the road of life because of a mistake. So why then do you want to give up because you have made a mistake?

Unwise people avoid mistakes but wise people learn from their mistakes.

Learning from your mistakes will inspire you to change and improve your life. You don't learn from mistakes by avoiding them; you only learn by embracing them. One thing I have personally learnt from my mistakes in life is that, they enable me to OBSERVE, LEARN, DEVELOP, EDUCATE, DECIDE, and become RESPONSIBLE. If you add the first letters of each aforementioned benefit, it will give you the word *O.L.D.E.R*. Mistakes should make you older!

We should be able to tell people not to shy away from making mistakes because in their mistakes lie the prospects for growth. Mistakes build confidence in us to achieve more and become better in life. People who make mistakes learn from them by responding to life differently and more positively. They do not live their lives anyhow. There are great lessons in mistakes. Don't avoid them; learn from them.

FIVE BENEFITS OF MISTAKES

There are a lot of benefits we can derive from our mistakes. These benefits help to reshape our attitudes towards life as we become more successful and relevant in society.

1. You become diligent

Mistakes bring out the best in us if we know how to cash in on them. We tend to work harder when we make mistakes. Most successful people get committed to what they have set before them and do everything possible to achieve it because they know how painful mistakes can be. Hence, they put all their efforts into everything they do when working on their ideas just to ensure that they hit their target. Mistakes make you diligent.

2. You learn to be patient

When you haven't made a mistake in life, you think everything is about rush, rush, and rush. You become hasty about life. However, when you make mistakes and learn from them, you become more cautious and careful about the way you carry yourself and live your life. It helps you to appreciate the fact that nothing is gained through rushing but patience.

You can microwave porridge but you cannot do that with success. My late grandmother once said, "A patient dog can only eat a fat bone". This statement has taught me to be patient in life and never rush to be successful overnight. With patience, sustainable success can be achieved.

3. You become focused and determined

Successful individuals are more determined and focused to achieve something in life. This is because they have learnt from their mistakes and know how to avoid repeating the same mistakes over and over again. Mistakes also help you to remain resolute, dedicated, and determined by sticking to your goals in your pursuit of success.

It takes great effort and determination to overcome the barriers of failure. This only becomes possible when you learn to identify, accept your mistakes and have the mindset to learn. Be like the postage stamp on an envelope which never leaves the envelope even if it arrives at the wrong address. You've got to stick until you reach your destination in life. For you to achieve success in life, you should be ready to be dedicated to pursue and improve upon yourself no matter the number of times you make mistakes. This is how your dreams and goals are achieved. Never allow anything or anyone to stand before you in the pursuit of your dreams.

4. You learn to plan ahead

Another benefit of mistakes is that you become an effective planner. People who learn to plan have learnt that failing to plan results in failure and disappointment. Mistakes make us more proactive and organized. Don't take things for granted; develop the habit to plan, work towards your goals, and become successful. Nothing works and gets a man to the finish line like good planning, accompanied with corresponding action. Plans help us to build internal confidence and belief in our abilities to achieve anything we set our minds to do.

Sometimes, we lack boldness to try something simply because we have filled our minds with the idea that we will fail and become a laughing stock. This stops us from believing in our strengths and rather focus on our weaknesses just because we do not want to be mocked or laughed at. I put it to you that regardless of the number of times you have failed, you have the power to keep trying until you succeed. Don't give up.

It was Michael Jordan who confessed, *"I've missed more than 9,000 shots in my career. I've lost almost 300 games. Twenty-six times I've been trusted to take the game-winning shot and missed. I've failed over and over and over again in my life. And that is why I succeed."*[1] Just like Jordan, you need to start changing your attitude towards mistakes. You will always make mistakes on your way to success but you have valuable lessons to learn if you faint not. Step up and keep up. You are destined to succeed through your mistakes.

---

1 https://www.forbes.com/quotes/11194/

You may have made the mistake by picking the wrong pair of shoes for a ballroom dance; you may have gotten into the wrong bus or train. What now? Would you find another way to deal with it and learn a vital lesson from your mistakes? Well, this is life!

5. Mistakes help you to choose your friends wisely

Sometimes, we get into wrong associations or relationships with people we do not like or jobs we don't even want to do. It does not mean we should give up and throw in the towel. Not everyone is lovable or caring. If you think you have made a mistake by getting into the wrong association, you can only get out from it but it should not prevent you from trying another relationship that's in your best interest. Know that you cannot change people by yourself. Never allow negative people to pollute your mind, environment or change the direction of your purpose in life.

Live to learn and learn from your mistake.

04

THE ART OF DELEGATION

(PASSING ON THE BATON)

Learning how to bring out the best in others is one of the most important things you will ever do as a mentor. Once you have confidence in yourself and feel you are on your way to becoming the person you want to be, it's time to focus on bringing out the best in others by learning to delegate some level of power to your mentees or subordinates as the case may be.

Our ability to believe in the success of our mentees or protégés as mentors will help mentees know that we genuinely want to see them do well and are committed to helping them. When this happens, they begin to believe they can accomplish what you give them to do.

Most people do well to maximize their potentials when they are given the opportunity to do so. You can never get the best in others if you deny them the opportunity to use their talents, skills, and knowledge to add value to their community.

This is why delegation is very crucial in bringing out the best in others. No one is without skills or talents, but for those talents and skills to be maximized, people need platforms to deploy them in order to be at their best.

Therefore, if we as leaders, managers or coaches want to benefit from the talents of others, we will need to learn to pass on the baton for others to do what they can do with their skills, talents, and knowledge.

To help bring out the best in people, we must pass on the baton to them and give them the opportunity to experience victory and success.

Passing on the baton implies delegating a role to people. If we want to see others do well, we need to examine how we delegate tasks to them. Without delegation, we cannot see how best one can be effective.

Whatever vision or dream we have, we must learn to train others and trust them enough to delegate some tasks to them. This is how they will feel useful in life and use all their skills to produce effective results for their future.

Passing on the baton is one of the most important decisions anyone will ever make in bringing the best out of others as this shows how much we value and cherish the distinct talents and abilities of the people we are trying to help grow.

Passing on the baton is a process in which an opportunity, platform or access is given an individual with the confidence that he or she can deploy his or her ability to get a task done under supervision.

Therefore, from the above, it is possible to justify that passing on the baton is how we can replicate ourselves in others to bring stability and effectiveness to our organizations as it is in a relay race whereby an athlete hands a baton to the next athlete in order to carry on the race or finish it. Without delegation, long-term success in any establishment can't be achieved.

"No executive has ever suffered because his subordinates were strong and effective." **– Peter Drucker**

Failure to delegate is a common weakness in many leadership structures and this is typical of selfish leaders who don't want to see others grow and develop. Every forward-thinking leader, mentor, or coach takes delight in passing on what they know to others and delegating them to function whilst they watch and direct them to be the best.

Greatness or success in business, ministry, organizations, and entrepreneurship must not stop with the leader when he or she is gone.

People get better at the things they do passionately when tasks are delegated to them and they are challenged to take on responsibilities. Although some may make mistakes along the way, they grow and learn from such mistakes and rise above the challenges of life.

It is our ability to bring others under our wings as leaders, mentors and coaches in order to help them through the hurdles of life that endears people to us. Like children, the people in our lives need patience, motivation, and understanding to sustain their drive towards excellence.

We cannot effectively influence the people we don't have patience for. They will need our full attention in order for them to grow, develop, and impact their world. A great mentor is one who discovers hidden treasures in others and releases them to deploy their talents so as to influence and make positive impact on others.

Leadership in organizations becomes stagnant when sustainability is not ensured through capacity-building and delegation. The future of every leader lies in the people they delegate to or duplicate themselves into. When we delegate or pass on the baton to others, they get inspired and motivated to grow and take responsibility.

This is how progress is achieved and maintained in any organization that has the future in mind. This is why it is essential that we cultivate the habit of sharing authority and responsibilities among the people we mentor, lead, and coach so that they can develop.

It is imperative to know that people are different and have different ways of dealing with things. However, this does not prevent us from learning to delegate power to them.

Although we all like things done in a specific way, we must not deny others the opportunity to learn how certain things are done or carried out.

Whenever we fail to delegate responsibilities to people, we create room for them to fail. The only way for people to develop skills and improve is by doing. This is how they are able to bring value to the table.

No one is a superman; the best way to be the best is to delegate to others

It is very important that we identify one or two people in our organizations who we can trust and have confidence in to do the things we do without fear.

Delegation promotes and builds confidence in others and takes away some burdens that we can afford to share especially when we are already overwhelmed with other responsibilities.

Part of being a good coach or mentor to others is our understanding of the people we mentor and coach. We are able to know their individual strengths, weaknesses, and abilities. This helps us to delegate tasks to them based on their capability to deploy effectively, coaching them appropriately with the right skills.

People will always be people. They will always need our encouragement, motivation, inspiration, empowerment and support to be at their best. We have to do everything to help them find the hidden treasures in them; develop the right passion, attitude, and discipline to become all they are on earth for. Don't deny them that opportunity.

By this, we are able to tailor what is best for them, building trust with them and entrusting them with the right knowledge and information for their development and growth.

Instead of taking advantage of, exploiting or abusing those under our wings, we can choose to put the relevant resources at their disposal in a bid to build them up and allow them to make the best use of their time, skills, and talent to reach their full potential.

Our ability to properly delegate to the people we are developing will go a long way to increase trust and commitment; thereby inspiring them to improve their productivity at any level. Therefore, we should not be afraid to delegate to others.

NO ONE RUNS A RELAY RACE ALL BY THEMSELVES AND WINS

Mentoring or coaching others is like running a relay race with others; in order to win, one must be able to pass on the baton. Delegation is like passing the baton to others to finish what we have started. This motivates them to play their part in winning the race.

This therefore means that, running a relay without passing on the baton (delegation) is tantamount to losing the race. Whenever we fail to pass on the baton to others, not only do we fail them, but we fail ourselves and the whole team. Interestingly, many people have not been able to enrich the world with what they have on the inside because no one has given them the opportunity to use their talents and live out their purpose.

In order to hew the best out of others, it is prudent that we set time aside to train and delegate tasks to them. Until we do this, the people we lead and influence will scarcely ever find the chance to break free from the dependency syndrome. If we really want to bring out the best in others, we must do everything within our power to help them birth their talents, not bury them.

We need to instill in the people we lead a sense of the importance of their talents and how that has the potential to change and turn their lives around. We must encourage them to appreciate their talents, gifts, and skills and use same to bring glory to God.

They may be good at singing, writing, typing, painting, speaking, repairing, or baking. Whatever they are good at, let us begin to create an enabling environment to enable them use those talents to help others.

You must stand back and let others get on with what you have delegated to them. You must make it clear to whomever you delegate to that you are always available to support them.

Most importantly, ensure clarity in the instructions you give to those who take orders from you. Forthwith, you must be willing to address any form of setback or challenge that may arise.

Nothing they have is useless in God's hands. Their gift or talent is not useless. It is needed in the corner where they are. God is the source of their life and whatever He has blessed them with, He expects them to use it to bless the world. By so doing, the world can appreciate and worship Him.

Many people have failed in life because there hasn't been anyone available to train and mentor them to avoid the pitfalls of life. Many businesses are failing or have failed as a result of leaders failing to delegate some vital roles to those serving under them. The profit margin or chances of expansion get slimmer due to a leader's inability to teach and delegate others to manage the several moving parts they deal with.

In my three years at the university, I was elected as the student representative. Being a student representative combined with my studies was not fun at all. However, I played my role very well and ensured that my studies never suffered for it. Everything played out well simply because I identified students whom I trusted and delegated to work with me.

DELEGATION IN LEADERSHIP IS CRUCIAL FOR THE SUCCESS OF EVERY LEADER

It takes a great deal of faith in your followers or mentees to delegate tasks to them. Sadly, many don't even have faith in themselves let alone in others. Whenever we have trust issues, we limit our chances of getting others involved in what we do. We often do not delegate to others simply because we think they will fail and disappointment us. Lack of faith in others will prevent us from bringing out the best in them. Without faith in others, delegating to them will be a high mountain to surmount in leadership.

Our ability to have faith in others helps to encourage them to go out of their way to do the impossible.

It is our duty to have faith in the people we lead, mentor, and coach to enable them shine the light they have to get to where they really want to get in life.

Delegating to others helps assure them that you have faith in their ability, talents, and skills

They don't feel isolated, sidelined or rejected. People are like seeds. They can't grow and bear fruits in a day. They have to be nurtured into their dreams. So in order to help them get the best out of them, it is your interest in them that will also help you to know and identify the area(s) in which they need to grow. With compassion and understanding, you will be able to assist them to develop and grow.

This is why as we work hard to bring out the best in people, we are minded to have faith in them, delegate and allow them to use their talents in the capacity in which they really feel comfortable.

Doing this will raise their level to meet the standard and expectation we have set for them. Trusting and having faith in others ignites and sets them up for success.

People become very bold, assured, and energized in using their talents and gifting as we have faith in them.

If we want to continue to make positive impact on people with our lives, then we need to treat them well with respect and kindness so as to build their confidence and bring out the best in them. Every time we delegate responsibilities, we show them that we trust and have faith in them in being their best. This gives them a platform of confidence to grow and improve.

Delegation builds confidence in followers and mentees to improve and succeed in life

I learnt that the previous student representative didn't do well because he thought he could do everything by himself. Consequently, he failed the students and lecturers.

The hardest lesson I learnt as a student representative was this; to be able to bring out the best in others, one has to learn to delegate tasks to others and ensure they are confident and determined to follow through with your encouragement and motivation.

Whenever we secretly go back to perform tasks we delegated to others, we create an atmosphere of confusion and doubt in the hearts and minds of the people; thereby destroying our faith and trust in them.

People will always be our greatest assets in life if we really want to achieve with them; however, having the wrong one in your life is like having a bone stuck in between your teeth. Getting to know the right people in your life and your way to success helps you to tap relevant information you need. The right people will encourage and motivate you. They do everything to increase your own value and worth when you pass on the baton to them.

Whatever you do in life, remember that people will always be people and you must be yourself to overcome discouragement. Some may pose as discouragers, but you need to take hold of yourself and remain encouraged at all times so as to succeed and win with people.

You can become a great and influential person if you learn to delegate to others and release them to run with the baton of life. You will be able to use the power and influence you have to push others into their next level; helping them to make the positive impact they are also designed to make on the people around them. Don't deny them the baton, release it and let your protégés run with it. This is how you win, achieve, and succeed with people.

05

BE A MENTOR, NOT A MANIPULATOR

Beside every achiever is a mentor. There is no greatness without mentorship or coaching. Mentors or coaches play a significant role in shaping us for our destiny. The wise King Solomon once said, there is nothing new under the sun. There is no height we can attain which has never been attempted. One can only stand tall thanks to the foundation that others have put in place. Indeed, we are all products of others' successes. No one becomes great or achieves anything without the support, push, motivation or encouragement of others.

We cannot mentor the people we are not ready to connect with. Our connection determines our influence and impact. For you to lead others more effectively, you will have to connect with them emotionally, mentally and spiritually.

Relationships ought to bring about mutual benefit. It is important that the parties involved value and appreciate each other so as to find a common ground to the top. When you rightly connect with the people you lead, it is easier for them to come to your level and properly relate with you.

Sometimes, mentoring others in a church setting can be one of the most challenging areas in mentorship. Members become too familiar with one another such that they fail to respect the position of the mentor and downplay the leader's authority.

When people become overly familiar with you, they undermine and devalue the impact you can make on them. As a mentor, it is very important to have standards by which you live your life and mentor others. It is therefore necessary that we also make ourselves available to mentor others if we really want to extract the best in them.

We should be prepared to share some of our life's experiences with others which will go a long way to inspire or propel them into becoming all that they want to become.

As mentors or coaches, we are there to guide, lead, direct and motivate people to achieve whatever they have set their minds to. We are supposed to build people up rather than manipulate or pull them down. People should be able to trust or have faith in us; to be convinced that we are there to help them grow and succeed in life.

Mentorship doesn't only involve a one-on-one setup. It goes beyond that. It can equally be done in the context of a group or team. There is no limit to the number of people you would like to have in your mentorship group. However, in order to be effective, you have to pick a limited number of people for mentorship.

With the current situation we live in as a society, one has to think beyond mentoring others and ensure that the mentorship he or she is providing is measurable, cost-effective, and makes a great difference on the group. We need to reflect on our practices as it relates to grooming people for the best outcomes.

Without the required skills, mentoring cannot be effective or sustainable. For example, you cannot mentor the people you don't pay attention to or listen to. Listening is an aspect of effective communication. This means that without good communication skills, mentorship will be an uphill task.

You will be amazed to know that people will only enjoy you speak about your success if you pay attention to them. So, if we aim at getting the best out of others, we need to learn to pay attention to their needs.

We must be ready to share ideas that will enforce or activate the winning spirit or attitude in our mentees. This takes time, patience, and collaboration between the mentor and his or her mentee(s).

People do well in business, sports, education, marriage etc. when they are mentored in the right direction without prejudice. We must go to great lengths to spur and inspire our mentees, students, clients, children, team members, or group without being coerced. When we invest time and effort in mentoring others, it enhances their personal growth, knowledge, and desire to develop and succeed in life.

Thus, we are role models for these people and we are expected to display positive behaviors. Every mentor understands that to be effective in his or her role, he or she needs to be dependable, engaged, authentic, and tuned in to the needs of his or her protégées (mentees).

As mentors, we have the ability to mold or break our team, mentees or organizations depending on our attitude, mindset, and character.

It is our sole responsibility to help followers discover their potentials and guide them to take steps to maximize their purpose for living. This is how we get to draw forth the best that's embedded in them so that they can add value to society.

Interestingly, we live in the age where talking about leadership is not enough; our walking the talk through effective mentoring is needed to develop others into agents of change. As mentors, our desires should gear towards blazing the trail for the people we lead; we should aspire to help them chart a good course for their lives. As they begin to fulfil their purpose, the world will feel their impact in tangible ways.

We can't mentor others successfully without building a strong relationship with them. We all know the idiomatic expression that "It takes two to tango". This means that to help bring the best out of others, they have to develop the desire to be mentored. They must see the need to be helped as they take on their life journey. That you see greatness in someone doesn't mean you can trigger that seed of greatness to sprout without their collaboration.

Whoever wants to be mentored must value and appreciate your knowledge and experiences in order for you to help birth the greatness in them. This is how you can share relevant knowledge, experience, and advice with them in order to build leadership skills and improve their communication skills.

When we mentor others, not only do we share relevant information or knowledge and skills with them, but also our own experience and wisdom become the fulcrum on which they pitch their professional attitudes, personal attributes, and personal growth and development.

When we mentor people, we provide them with lenses to see and learn things differently. We help people to broaden their scope of thinking to the end that they can think outside the box and engage with others with similar interests and desire to work towards significance.

Mentoring is crucial in reshaping and guiding the future of our leadership as it provides a leeway for upcoming or emerging leaders in ministry, business, and entrepreneurship.

In the business world, mentorship plays a cardinal role in many inventions. It becomes the platform for productivity by which those on the front-line share their experiences and knowledge with others in the same business in order to help them improve in their business know-how. The importance of mentorship in nursing, for example, can't be overlooked.

As I noted earlier, we are all products of someone's success and greatness. In nursing, this has been the case. Mentors within the nursing field have provided and continue to provide platforms for new nurses. Through these platforms, they educate, orient, and usher them into the healthcare profession. These mentors provide an environment for new nurses or students to make strides in their personal and professional development. This promotes and enhances self-confidence as it relates to adherence to standard practice, all ethical issues considered.

There are many great nurses out there doing their best in caring for their patients because someone in the past availed himself or herself to be a great mentor to them.

Granted, from time to time, we hear bad news about some nurses who abuse or ill-treat their patients. However, it is also necessary to highlight the great roles mentors play in changing the negative notion of this noble profession by creating a positive environment for learning and nurturing good character and attitudes among new nurses to ensure that the nobility of the nursing profession is not compromised.

For us to be able to extract the best in others, we must be interested in their professional development and be willing to share information about their career path and their future plans with them.

We must serve as an information source even as we provide them with guidance, motivation, emotional support, and role modeling in the things they desire to become in life.

We cannot effectively mentor those we are not interested in. We ought to show interest in what others do in order to know exactly what they need to grow and develop in business, ministry, or leadership. Equipped with such awareness, we can better help them explore careers, set goals, develop contacts, and identify and take advantage of needful resources.

For us to help bring forth the best in others, we must be ready to help change the perception they have about themselves and create a sense of positive vibes in them about how they can take charge of their own lives for good.

Sometimes, even the minor adjustments we trigger in the course of mentoring others can make a huge difference in their personal development. As mentors, we should be intentional about moving the lives of those under our care forward. This helps them to continue to move forward toward their goals and dreams because they will recognize and realize the best in themselves.

As I have already mentioned, mentorship provides valuable support for mentees at critical points in their life. It provides the bridge by which mentees cross to reach their ultimate goals and purpose in life. Without effective mentoring, many of us wouldn't be where we all are today.

A mentor represents some of life's greatest lessons in a condensed form. You are able to observe, learn, relearn, and unlearn when you are walking in the footsteps of a good mentor. Mentorship helps you to steer clear of the ambushes on the highway of success. It helps you to build on helpful, practical advice; donates a sense of direction such that you can become more and do more. Mentees are able to develop or make use of their skills to pursue their goals, vision, and purpose.

As mentors, we are there to make a difference in the lives of our mentees. Although it can be very difficult at times, we should be able to take control of our emotions and take giant steps to make that positive difference in the people we want to help improve.

We should have a strong belief in the people we are mentoring, acknowledging that we were once in their shoes and create room for them to augment their quality of life. Our ability to inspire, motivate, encourage, empower, and transform them will generate the force to get the best out of our mentees.

In order to make a good impression on our mentees, we should be quick to identify the impending hurdles, obstacles or challenges on their way and provide the needed support to help them overcome and be their best. No matter the challenges and hurdles along the way, it is important that we take responsibility to ensure that our mentees get the best in life to become all they are here on the planet for.

Personally, I have no doubt that some mentees find it very difficult to cooperate with us when it comes to making certain decisions. Notwithstanding, we should not give up on them.

Some may give 1001 reasons as to why they don't feel like doing or taking some steps to see their dreams come true. We should also give them 999 reasons why we think they are more than able to hit their targets.

It is our responsibility to let them understand that all great achievers go through challenging times but they never give up in the pursuit of their dreams. Such people take full responsibility towards their goals and dreams to fulfil their life's aspirations.

Having a great skill without good mentors makes your skills meaningless. This is why we need to be patient with people in order to mentor and help chisel the best out of them.

Without great mentors in the life of Usain Bolt, Cristiano Ronaldo, Gareth Bale, Mark Zuckerberg (Co-Founder and CEO, Facebook) Richard Branson (Founder, Virgin Group) Bill Gates (Founder and Technology Advisor, Microsoft), the disciples of Jesus Christ, and Timothy, they would have made a shipwreck of their professions.

As mentors, we are the mirrors through whom others see their future. They see themselves in the things we do and tell them to do. When they are faced with difficult issues, disappointment, and hopelessness, they tap courage, consolation, and strength from us.

When our mentees feel unmotivated, frustrated, and discouraged about life, we must be able to brighten their corners and bring hope in their hopeless situations.

Sometimes, most of the people we mentor struggle with low self-esteem due to past abuses, failures or mistakes and are not motivated to develop themselves. Some see themselves as useless and develop a negative outlook on life.

In this regard, a mentor must take on the task of helping them develop their positive self-image. Self-perception plays a crucial part in the way one approaches life.

Self-image is so powerful in changing our behavior and inspires us to value who we are in this world. Although many people don't realize how important and powerful their self-image is, it is our duty as mentors to help them discover this and help them believe in who they are.

Although sometimes it may seem easier for some of these mentees to give up on their dreams, aspirations, and goals, we must do everything within our power to provide strength and support to help sustain their fire. Most often, what people need in life are not the obvious things like money and sex but motivation and encouragement to pursue a cause in life. This is why mentors come in to provide the avenue for their mentees to get back on their feet to achieve undeniable success.

Let's step out there to help nurture talents in others as mentors especially if we notice that someone has a talent that they aren't putting to use. We should be able to draw their attention to it and encourage them to put it to use. We should be able provide or offer suggestions of where they may go to learn more.

"A MENTOR IS SOMEONE WHO ALLOWS YOU TO SEE THE HOPE INSIDE YOURSELF." — OPRAH WINFREY

As mentors, we are to motivate and reassure the people we mentor to see the light at the end of the tunnel. We are to provide them with the platform for them to see greatness in themselves even in failures by keeping their dreams and aspirations alive.

There are many ways to make a positive impact on others as mentors and we can act as career advisors and advocates, helping to improve how people treat their health, job, relationships and social life; thereby making sure they get the best in life.

If the person we are mentoring is constantly showing interest in soccer, for example, we should get them signed up for a soccer academy to help harness that skill in them.

We shouldn't be selfish as mentors to sit on the talents of those we mentor knowing very well that when we push them further, they could be the next Ronaldo, Pele, Mike Tyson, Amir Khan, Messi or Mohammed Ali.

As mentors, it is our duty to identify and help nurture greatness in others. Mentorship is not about self; it is about selfless service. We owe a duty to the society where we have been placed as leaders to live an exemplary life.

When mentors prioritize the needs of their mentees, it creates a culture of growth. We need more selfless leaders in our society who have a generational mindset.

Mentors are supposed to be the light to shine in the path of their followers so that, they can see clearly what they are meant to do and live to the maximization of their destiny. It takes an extraordinary and effective mentor to turn ordinary and visionless mentees into extraordinary, outstanding and effective leaders who would make impact in the world.

Mentors are very crucial in the rediscovery of the next crop of leaders who will reshape the direction and vision of society, and to make changes in the lives of others. That can only be possible if mentors are willing to align with the purpose and characteristics of effective mentorship.

Society has become stagnant and retarded in the area of mentors especially in churches, ministries, businesses, institutions, colleges, families, relationships, marriages and many more because of the lack of forward-thinking leadership. This can only be possible if we go out and support people with great talents out there.

The purpose and value of mentorship is not limited to positional privileges, but in steps taken to transform followers into great and impactful leaders.

GREAT MENTORS PRODUCE OTHER ACHIEVERS

Steve Jobs mentored Mark Zuckerberg (Facebook) into who he is now. When Steve Jobs died in 2011, Mark Zuckerberg wrote a heart-moving tribute thanking him for being a great and inspiring mentor to him because of the relationship they shared.

Oprah Winfrey was also mentored by Maya Angelou; Michael van der Peet mentored Mother Teresa, Christian Dior mentored Yves Saint-Laurent, Warren Buffett mentored Bill Gates, Steven Spielberg mentored J.J. Abrams, and Mahatma Gandhi indirectly mentored Nelson Mandela through his books and writings.

Michelle Robinson (MICHELLE OBAMA) was Barack Obama's mentor for many years and she is behind his great achievements;

Sir Freddie Laker mentored and helped turn Richard Branson into who he is.

There are great and inspiring people out there with special and unique stories that need our support as mentors to develop the hidden gifts and skills in them like such as was the case with Bill Gates who created Microsoft. Bill Gates had a hidden talent for a long time as an amateur programmer. He was a very passionate computer programmer at an early age. He was mentored and encouraged to pursue his passion and he did. Because he followed his passion, you and I have the privilege to benefit from the works of his hands today.

As mentors, we hold in our hands the keys to the success or failures of our mentees. This is the more reason why it is important for us to build solid relationships with the people we mentor. The world will become a great place if we all identify and provide mentorship to those who need a hand.

Let's be effective mentors, not monsters or manipulative individuals who use mentees for personal gain and deny them the possibility of self-development and significance.

06

BE SINCERE AND HONEST WITH PEOPLE

No one gets the best out of others without first being sincere with them. Sincerity plays a significant role in helping us get the best in others especially when they rely on us for their next level in their business, career, marriage, etc.

In fact, it is the bedrock for effective communication. People connect and relate well with us when we remain sincere and honest with them. Being sincere with others creates the platform for them to build trust and believe in us because we don't try to cover up lies or pretend we are something we are not.

Being sincere simply means living a life void of deceit, pretense, and hypocrisy. People are able to give out their best when we are sincere with them through in our motives and actions.

Our relationships are improved as we begin to learn new things about the people, team members, mentees, co-workers, colleagues, and business partners we interact with. Being sincere is important in building others and transforming them into the best they can be. Nobody likes to be deceived or lied to. It therefore follows that if we want others to trust us and commit themselves to the things we expect them to do, then we need to be sincere and honest with them at all times.

When we are sincere with people, they always desire to be with us, relate with and associate with us anytime without having doubts about us or negative opinions about our character or attitude.

We are able to enjoy a large circle of friends, partners, and associates who will like to share ideas with us which can go a long way to add value to, and change our lives.

You can never build a solid and genuinely happy team if you don't understand the value of sincerity. Getting the best out of others can only be possible when we remain sincere and honest with them.

Most people are likely to repose trust in a sincere person without nursing the fear of being taken for granted. Our friendly attitude towards others is another dignified feature of our sincerity.

SINCERITY AFFIRMS TRUE LOVE AMONG TEAM MEMBERS

When we are sincere with people, we tend to show them compassion and love. We must make it a point of duty not to treat our subordinates and/ co-workers anyhow. We ought to reassure and encourage those we lead or mentor to become their best in life.

People are the greatest asset to our next level and for us to bring the best out of them, we need to respect them and treat them as humans and not as objects.

Our attitude and character towards people must reveal our burning heart desire for their development and growth. We shouldn't say one thing and mean the other. We should be sincere in our words and actions. It's our sincerity that opens doors and knocks down barriers for us to bring out the best in others.

As a matter of fact, not everyone will like us for our sincerity. However, no one loves and follows a liar and a pretender. So, although not everyone will appreciate us for what we say or do, it is vital we remain sincere and make the effort to match our words with our actions.

Pretenders or insincere people are difficult to deal and relate with. Sadly, some people love to pretend just so they can feel good about themselves. Such people think that being real with others can seem offensive. This phenomenon gradually culminates into making them insincere in character and attitude. Such persons manifest many colors like the chameleon. They change their words and actions to please others. Consequently, they end up driving people away as others get to know their real nature with time.

AN INSINCERE PERSON IS NEVER TRUSTED OR BELIEVED

In order for us to develop others or help them grow, we need to remain truthful in our attitude, character and actions. People need to have faith in us as leaders, coaches, mentors, managers or preachers. But, it will take our courage to be sincere with them in truth and sincerity.

People will always want to be around us when we are sincere and honest with them. This gives us the latitude and liberty to improve their lives. We are to be agents of change to people, inspiring them to pursue a greater purpose and a vision for their lives; and the only way we can effectively achieve this is to be honest and sincere with them.

Sincerity enables us to lead and help others from our heart and not just with the hand. Those who lead from the heart don't try to manipulate, control, and intimidate people.

Insincerity or dishonesty makes us harsh, unreasonable, inconsiderate, and heartless in our relationships with people. When we deal with people in sincerity, it creates an atmosphere of security in our relationships

When we display sincerity, it demonstrates that we have a heart of integrity. Integrity speaks volumes about us as we strive to help others. When people see that we are sincere with them, they get inspired and motivated to be sincere and loyal to us without feeling that they are being used or taken for granted.

Sincerity breeds integrity in relationships

Sincerity creates room for faithfulness, commitment, and selflessness in protégés and enhances growth and productivity in business, ministry, and the church. Our character and words are the main things that reveal if we are controlling or caring.

Spending time with loved ones shows how caring and loving we are and that cannot be possible without our being sincere to ourselves and then to others.

Sincerity enables us to touch the hearts of everyone around us by our feelings, intents, and presentations. Whatever we do or say must bear an undertone of genuineness. We must be sincere with our approval to the people around us and maintain it against all odds. Never say good things about any one and not mean it. When we do that, it betrays our relationship with them. This is a truism.

Most sincere people always have great and loyal people around them. They have honest people around them simply because they themselves have proven to be honest and sincere.

People become transparent and open with us when we create room for sincerity and honesty among the people we desire to improve and develop. We are able to listen to the needs of the people around us, doing everything possible to foster effective communication.

Sincerity and honesty must be our watchwords if we hope to set a good example for our followers, mentees, members, workers, etc.; an example that can be emulated.

When we fail to be honest and sincere with others, they can't trust us at any level. Failing to be honest destroys the respect and value people have for us which then affects their relationships with us and hampers our collective growth and success.

In business, dishonesty on the part of a company has serious and damaging consequences on its future. Dishonesty reduces the value of such company and creates a poor reputation among business partners and prospective customers.

In my profession as a Public Health worker, it is required of every healthcare professional to ensure that they remain honest in dealing with patients. Patients have a right to receive as much information about their care and condition as they require and such information must be given in honesty.

We are mandated as healthcare professionals to provide adequate and relevant information to patients when demanded; under no circumstance must we provide wrong information to service users as that will be deemed as dishonesty and closes the dialogue between the patient and healthcare team, leading to the absence of respect.

Effective leadership is about integrity. You will be surprised to know that many people fail this test which affects their leadership and changes the perception followers have about them. The question is: what is this integrity about? Some schools of thought believe that integrity plays a vital role in determining the future of any leader and the absence thereof leads to unavoidable failure.

People always want those they can easily trust and be confident around. They are looking for people who can remain truthful and honest even in the face of great temptation. Trust is gained through honesty. Our level of honesty determines the level of loyalty we attract from others. This is how we are able to help bring the best out in others.

If we want to continue to bring out the best in others, we need to be aware of the attitude we display around people. Also, it is important to bear in mind that society will demand integrity, sincerity, and honesty from us.

You will be amazed to know that people who do well in bringing out the best in others have taken the pain to cultivate the spirit of honesty and sincerity by developing and working on their self-awareness, adhering to moral principles and effectively communicating truthfully with the people they lead.

People who want to help reshape and mold others must learn to lead themselves first before thinking of leading others. This helps them to discover through the eyes of others whom they are inspired by and to gain more knowledge about the kind of person they want to be. Doing this may help them avoid certain mistakes committed by others who may have gotten them in trouble or brought their leadership to question.

Just as every seed needs the right soil to grow and every tree needs the right atmosphere to enable it bear fruits, so is the art of helping people to be at their best. So, to be able to bring out the best in others, we must be confident about our position in supporting them to develop and grow into their purpose.

Leading people with integrity empowers them to develop unshakable commitment to the leader and gives them a sense of security. Everybody wants security and it is the leader's responsibility to create that around the followers by fostering a culture of transparency.

People who serve or lead with integrity and sincerity always look for an opportunity to motivate and empower everyone under their influence to become their best and become beneficial to society.

Such people don't allow their self-interest to cloud their focus or prevent them from identifying the need for developing others. They have the heart of compassion and vision for individual followers and not just the few who give monetary gifts to draw the leader's attention to them.

People may want to change you into what they want and think, but you must be like the cocoon. Don't be moved by the challenges of life but let your life challenge the situations around you. The cocoon knows what it wants to be like so it does not allow just anything to change its genetic makeup.

Integrity is the catalyst for effectiveness

It is important that you really know what you want and go out for it regardless of the pressures and challenges around you. You alone know what you want and how you can get it. Step out of your shell of fear and make that thing a reality in your life.

Being around the fire is different from being in it. Mostly, people will judge you by what you say or how you look. They do this irrespective of the fact that they remain clueless as it relates to your real life experiences. It is therefore wise for you to turn to the one who understands you better than you understand yourself – the Maker of heaven and earth. He promised us that even when we go through the fire and water, He will be with us.

Don't lose hope in helping others become their best because people are relying on you to change their life. No matter what others say about you or the manner in which they treat you on the account of your uniqueness, stay different in a positive way and make the difference by getting rid of every form of pretense. Your personal relationship with God, not men, is what determines your revelation from God. Dare to be different. Even if an eaglet is set in the midst of a multitude of chicks, it will still be spotted by its mother. Stay true to who you are and be content with the people the Lord has blessed you with to mentor, nurture and develop. Until you remain different from the masses, your uniqueness and authenticity will not be seen and valued. Don't conform to the standards and notions of the people around you.

Note this: you can't be like everyone else and expect to be treated differently. If you live as a photocopy of others, how do you expect your authenticity and uniqueness to be appreciated, valued and respected? Nothing of value comes from imitation; only originality produces value. Be original; be true to yourself and never allow the hypes and the unreasonable expectations of people turn you into something you are not.

Begin to believe in yourself and never allow the voices of others to stop you from speaking. If you fail to show up, it will be hard for you to be heard. Nothing in this life is greater than you. You are born a winner and winners do not bow down to failure but step up to challenge everything that poses a threat to their success.

Be focused in life and live your authentic life. You can never achieve anything in life without being a person of focus. Remain determined and dedicated to your cause in life until you achieve or attain it.

Avoid comparing your leadership styles with others. Successful and influential people don't compare themselves with others but they learn from them and remain sincere with others. Comparing yourself with others will only enslave you. You are unique and you must hold on to what you have that makes you unique and authentic in this life.

The world may not understand or believe in you, but God knows and understands you. Keep believing in Him regardless. I challenge you to be different in everything you do, say, post, and write. Nobody can ever be you but you. Dare to be different and authentic so you can help get the best out of others.

07

BELIEVE IN THEIR SUCCESS

The best thing that can happen to you is to have someone believe in you and the little efforts you make to succeed in life.

The road to success can be daunting and challenging, but it's far more rewarding when you have someone who believes in you and roots for you as you make your run.

However, when you have someone who doesn't believe in you but constantly finds ways to pick on your errors, mistakes and failure can be very devastating.

As humans, we love to know that others believe in us as it helps to increase our confidence and courage to excel in life.

As a matter of fact, not everyone will believe in you no matter how well you do. Therefore, it is important that you learn to believe in yourself as well as in others. Get interested in what others are doing well; encourage them and act in ways that depict your belief in them. Like children, people tend to grow and develop well when they see that an adult is interested in them and the little things they do. Irrespective of the odds your child is up against in school, he will do everything to rise above them if you believe in him and throw your weight behind him. This, in fact, builds some confidence in that child that he or she can achieve better next time.

To get the best out of others, we need to make them believe they can succeed. We should never be afraid to show them what our expectations are and what we believe is the best for them.

Like I mentioned earlier, we human beings love to hear that others believe in us. We like to hear that often and always looking forward to hearing it.

You can't get the best out of the people you talk down on and undermine. You must be mindful of this as dismissive and condescending language has the potential to destroy the hope and aspirations of the one being addressed.

It is our duty as coaches to ensure that we use the right words at the right time to the right people.

When people come to recognize that we are interested in them and their success, they will always go an extra mile to dedicate and commit themselves to discipline so as to be at their best.

Believing in people shows that you are ready and prepared to entrust them with a level of responsibility. It means that you are able to empower them to do their best in life without nursing the fear that you will crucify them for their mistakes.

To bring the best out in others, we must show a level of positive belief in them as it motivates them to get things done. Most often, others become bold, confident, and strong when they know that you believe in their decision-making ability and in their ability to knock out the challenges of life. No one knows or has it all, but believing in someone may cause them to feel they have conquered the world.

We don't have to wait for opportunities to publicly express our confidence in our mentees, associates or teammates. As you raise people up, show them your confidence in them and you will find how quickly they will live up to your expectations.

Believing in others is like using a bucket to draw water from a well. People do well when we show a level of belief in them. It actually instills confidence in them and raises their morale such that even if they fail, they know they can do better next time; thanks to the power of high expectations.

Many people can go great lengths to become successful in life only when we believe in them and motivate them. Such people become resilient and determined to keep trying until they achieve and succeed with their dreams and aspirations. Our belief in them gives them the platform to reach their full potential even when they cannot see the end of the road. Confidence grows when belief is at its peak. Fear and anxiety are the greatest enemies of confidence especially when we as coaches and mentors show no sign of trust in the abilities of the people we lead and mentor.

Fear and anxiety robs people of their confidence to excel and improve their life. This creates insecurity in many and zaps their self-esteem. However, when we show belief in those we lead and mentor, it creates a sense of security in them to develop their potentials by identifying their strengths and overcoming their weaknesses. They are able to develop and build confidence in relating with others without being afraid of rejection and intimidation especially when it comes to how others view them.

Being the kind of person who is interested in developing and building the potential of others, you need to acquire a range of skills. These include but are not limited to emotional intelligence and other interpersonal skills.

You must be keen to learn and become more knowledgeable, accountable, and competent in your approach in trusting and believing in the people you want to empower unto excellence. Believing in the success of others helps to stimulate further success in them. They become very inspired by the belief you have in them and are encouraged to do more. Such people will only surround themselves with the right people, right resources and foster enthusiasm in their peers.

It is also necessary to know that if we really want to bring out the best in others, we need to be careful not to impose ourselves on them. People need room to breathe and move. So, we should not be like a helicopter that hovers over them to patronize their space every time. Doing that can cause you to suffer burnout.

What is more, you will frustrate the people you lead, coach, or mentor. Many people have not been able to be their best in life simply because someone might have behaved like a hawk around them, putting fear in them from doing what they are able to do. Hence, they have remained in the same spot for many years and are not interested in venturing into new horizons to become their best in life.

Being a leader is not about avoiding mistakes, but learning and amending or correcting your mistakes as you make progress. This means that, you must be very accommodating as you deal with the people you lead; ensuring that you provide them with the required and necessary support to make it in life. I am in no way suggesting that we should support people who are engaged in fraudulent practices. Rather, we should do everything to show love and concern to the people we lead and to stand with them as they make positive decisions or take steps in making changes to correct their mistakes.

There is a constant need for mentors, coaches, and leaders to believe in the people they lead and mentor. If we don't have this belief in our mentees, then who else will?

When our mentees know and feel that we believe in them, it can make them feel that they can achieve anything and everything under the sun. They will also be more willing to put more effort into what they are doing.

We are all capable of believing in other people. So, we should strive to be consistent in showing belief in our protégés as self-esteem can be difficult to maintain without continuous reaffirmation.

There is no doubt that the people we mentor or coach will sometimes push us to the wall, forcing us to be disappointed in them. However, we should not allow that to stop us from believing in their abilities to turn things around.

Unless we believe in someone, we can't encourage them to excel

Believing in people puts them on the road of success against all odds, hurdles and discouragements. Their confidence develops and matures as they take baby steps towards their dream with diligence and responsibility in every action they take.

For people to be something different, they have to do something different and that will be possible when we show them we believe in them more than they can imagine.

When we believe in people, it provides a ladder on which they can climb to reach their full potential. Strength comes from belief. So when we believe in people, they find strength to carry on in the pursuit of their vision, dreams, and goals.

Self-doubt is the killer of dreams and aspirations. Many have thrown in the towel and forfeited their vision because they had no one to believe in them. So, if we want to empower them to regain the confidence in themselves, then we need to believe in them once again.

Life, indeed, can be a lonely journey at times, but having the right people in your life who actually believe in you can enable you to develop wings like an eagle to soar into greatness.

No one knows what tomorrow will bring. So, be ready to be there for others, encouraging and believing in them as they go through life's challenges. We can never know who will stand by us when the chips are down.

Believing in others shows we are ready to understand their perceptions about life and situations. Without belief, understanding others becomes very difficult. Understanding others is the most strategic way to position ourselves as midwives to help birth the best in them.

Nothing brings us joy and happiness like the people we believe and support to develop and deploy their talents. It helps them to communicate with us because they can see that we believe in them.

The greatest error you can make is to put others down with your words and attitude or to limit them from striving for success. On the contrary, if you can see the good in others and capitalize on it, they would be fired up to attempt the seemingly impossible.

Lack of belief breeds fear and failure in the people we want to empower

We should do everything to eradicate fear from the people we mentor so as to motivate them unto success. This is our number one responsibility if we want to see our protégés succeed. Achieving one's dreams can be very scary, but belief and encouragement make most feats achievable.

Many have failed in life, not that they don't know what to do, but because of the fear of failure. Fear has limited lots of people from doing the right things to achieve their goals.

This is why as mentors, we need to believe in our mentees so they can build that confidence to believe in themselves once again when they flunk.

One of the greatest responsibilities we all have is to support others in getting the best out of them; whether as parents, partners, friends, mentors, coaches or leaders.

People have far more to offer than we think or can imagine and the best way to help them bring out the best in them is to believe in their ability to do more than they are currently doing to maximize their potentials.

Our words and actions influence the people we hobnob with; either positively or negatively. This is why believing in them empowers them to excel beyond their limits.

As mentioned earlier, doubting people kills the spirit of aspiration in them. Their self-esteem, confidence and motivation fade away when we don't believe in them to achieve the best.

When we lack faith in people, they don't shine in their talents and skills. This gives them very little incentive to launch out into new horizons or initiatives.

However, when we believe in them and openly demonstrate to them that we have faith in their ability, they suddenly develop an unbeatable attitude and step out to scale the heights of glory.

BELIEVING IN SOMEONE IS PRICELESS

Most of the great men and women we see on television, hear on radio and follow on social media have or had someone who believed in them even when the world doubted their capabilities.

The greater the belief, the greater the expectations. You see, there is no way you will ever believe a child of 5 to drive a car. So, your expectation from the child will be limited. However, if that child grows into a teenager or adult and you have invested so much for his driving lessons, you can now expect him to drive safely without endangering himself or other road users.

This is why is it very necessary that we have some level of belief in people as it helps them to maximize their full potentials without fear of being mocked or ridiculed.

Believing in people challenges them to step up and keep up to the test of time. Time has a way of testing our purported abilities.

If we ever want to get out the best in others and help them add value to their communities, society, family and the world at large, then we need to believe in them even when they cannot see anything good in themselves. Be a believer in people, not a doubter. Yes, you can switch to the positive side and you can start right now!

08

BE A GOOD PLANNER

For you to help bring out the best in others, you must be a good planner. Planning is one of the most important tools we all need in order to chisel out the best in people. Without effective planning, we can never lead others safely to their destiny. Anyone who fails to plan ahead is bound to fail.

Whatever we are in the lives of others; be it a leader, mentor, coach, teacher, manager, or minister, it is very necessary we plan things around the people we lead. Leadership or mentorship demands planning and planning requires timing.

Most people who fail in their leadership positions are those who fail to adopt planning. Planning is the ability to prepare an order of action or steps to achieve a task. A leader who is effective in planning will achieve greatly with people and win with them.

When planning becomes our second nature, we are able to follow a pattern of lifestyle to improve or develop ourselves and the people with and/or under us.

A plan is like a map that leads or directs the movement of the leader to their desired destination. Without a road map, a journey becomes a frustrating adventure.

Mentors or leaders who are able to see how much progress they are making in leading and helping others to achieve a common vision are good planners.

Planning goes a long way to help us have a structured life to attain valuable outcomes with the people we mentor or coach. We are able to major on the majors and minor on the minors because we have planned effectively to avoid the danger of falling prey into unnecessary, unproductive, and unachievable ventures.

Good planning helps us to organize crucial meetings, attend to vital needs and spending time, money, or other resources wisely on the people we work with. Problems are easily identified and solved when a leader practices strategic planning. To achieve our potential and maximize resources, we must have planning as part of our daily routine.

A leader's vision thrives well on the wings of planning. It does not really matter how great a leader's vision is; if he fails to plan, he will surely fail to achieve that vision.

Effective planning helps to determine our ability to remain focused in organizing things so as to reduce waste of time and human capital within our organizations and households.

Some ministries, for example, are doing so well because the leader is committed to planning. When someone fails to plan for his members, followers, mentees, workers or team members, the effectiveness and success of that organization or ministry breaks down.

I have witnessed a businessman who had everything going on for him simply because he is very committed to planning. He customarily involves members of his team in the process of planning and deciding on the steps that will move the business forward.

However, as time went on and the business was on television, selfishness crept in and he stopped involving the leaders in decision-making and went about what he wanted and felt like doing. He even made it public that he did not consult his team players before making decisions in the business. He failed to plan meetings with his leaders and always left the business for the wife and children to run. Such a person is doomed to fail big time if he continues to think he is a superman.

Personally, I think that because that businessman lost the ability to plan effectively, the mission statement and vision of that business was not made plain and clear to other leaders and members of his team.

This prevented the members from understanding the bigger picture of that business. Because of that lapse, he began to fail to organize career development programmes and seminars for the workers.

Planning helps the leader to be more directive and structured; this way, followers, team members and other workers become more accountable and responsible for their actions and they contribute to developing and shaping the future of the business in question. Leaders, for example, who plan and plan well increase the performance of their leadership and maximize results.

PLANNING IS THE BENCHMARK OF EVERY EFFECTIVE LEADER

Without effective planning, our leadership will be questionable. So, we must live to plan and plan to lead in order to manage and help bring out the best in people.

We must be able to plan around the vision, policies and objectives of the organization we are leading so as to come up with diverse approaches for accomplishment.

The high side of planning is this: it enables us to make decisions or organize and establish measures and put systems in place through which activities are arranged, and coordinated.

Planning can take different shapes and forms and it is our determination and commitment to be effective in our role as mentors, coaches and leaders that will determine the success of our contribution in the lives of others.

When we plan as leaders, managers or mentors, we are able to anticipate potential problems and expect success from the people we lead. Without effective planning, we cannot build a sustainable future with the people in our lives.

It is however vital that anyone who wants to lead others effectively and bring out the best in them learns the art of planning in order to help those under him or her and set priorities for themselves.

Undoubtedly, some leaders have succeeded in planning strategically for their team and have been able to grow their business with the few leaders they work with from scratch. For any ministry or organization to move forward and achieve more, the leader must learn to plan around those he or she leads. Under no circumstance should a leader think he is self-made and can achieve the overriding organizational goal alone.

Most often, leaders who think and behave like loners end up losing their key members or leaders and also limit the morale and enthusiasm of other potential leaders who could have stepped in to boost the performance of the business especially in the area of human capacity building. It is important to note however that people who take their time to plan well around others achieve greater results in life with the people they lead.

The Bible rightly records in Habakkuk 2:2 that, *"Then the Lord answered me and said: 'Write the vision and make it plain on tablets, that he may run who reads it.'"* It is important that we understand and concretize the purpose of planning. Planning mustn't be an abstract subject. It should be made practical for the people we lead and want to influence so that they can understand the vision and "run" with it.

Our plans must be broken down into short-, medium-, and long-term achievable units. Each of these must lead to the next. Let's take a practical look at how to go about setting these goals.

Long-term plans

Your long-term goals set the agenda for the life of your organization. Long-term plans span from 10 to 20 years. In the next ten to twenty years, where would you, your ministry, your organization, your members, your followers, your team, etc. be?

Many people leave planning for the long haul to chance. They believe that whatever will be, will be. But we have found that that mantra is not true. Whatever will be is what you plan for and precipitate with the right actions. If you plan with the long-term in mind and you work towards it, you are sure to enjoy the fruits. A wise man once said that the best people are those who have the future planned. Don't live for the short-term. Live with the long-term in mind as well.

As mentors or coaches, we need to have a long-term plan on how we want to have our ministry or organization positioned, and the various ways we seek to improve ourselves and our team. If we plan these well and have them well written out, and work at them with all diligence, we will meet the future with smiles.

For example, let's say our long-term goal for our church organization for the next twenty years is to increase our numerical strength by ten thousand members; we want to own our own mega auditorium that could hold thirty thousand members at a time, and have at least fifty branches across the nation.

This may look daunting but when we break it all down into medium- and short-term goals, we could achieve and, perhaps, exceed them.

Medium-term plans

The medium-term plan isn't any separate from the long-term. The medium-term works to fit into the long-term. With our long-term goal of increasing our numerical strength to ten thousand, put up our own mega auditorium, and establish at least fifty branches across the nation, we will need to further break them down into medium-term plans. We need to ask: in order to achieve our long-term plans, what are the medium-term actions we need to take within the next five to ten years to achieve our grand plans? Here, we could say, in the next five to ten years, we will identify twenty states where we would send evangelists to evangelize massively and plant churches.

Also, we will evangelize massively within our own state because we are set on increasing our numerical strength to ten thousand members.

Again, for us to put up our own auditorium, we will employ the services of real estate agents to get a parcel of land for us within our state. When we spell out these clearly and set timelines to them, we are forced to take action. Before we know it, we are well on our way to achieving our grand plans.

Short-term plans

Short-term plans are what we intend on doing from today to the next five years or less to help us achieve our ultimate long-term plans. As we have seen, our short- and medium-terms must fit well into our long-term plans.

At no point should our short- and medium-term plans differ from our long-term plans. Short-, medium-, and long-term plans work like a jigsaw. They all need to fit in to create the ideal picture we have in mind.

For our long-term goals of increasing our numerical strength to ten thousand members, building a mega auditorium that could hold thirty thousand members at a time, and establish fifty branches across the nation, we will need to start taking specific steps today, tomorrow, and the days after to help us achieve these goals. By no means would we want to establish our own auditorium and channel the chunk of our financial resources into major projects that have nothing to do with building the said auditorium.

To establish fifty branches across the nation, if we have a lack of evangelists or church planters, we need to train more of them to help us realize this goal. I would like to stress here that setting goals this way mustn't be a reserve for corporations, businesses, ministries, and teams. It should be extended to the individual.

The Bible highly recommends setting goals as we saw in Habakkuk 2:2. The greatest achievers, be they individuals or organizations, are the greatest planners and doers!

SETTING GOALS

As we saw previously, we have long-, medium-, and short-term plans written down. Setting of goals refers to the various steps to achieving those plans. We can have those plans without having the step-by-step approach to achieving them.

It's similar to a mathematics problem. It doesn't matter what the answer may be; you will need to go through a series of steps to get to the final answer. Goals serve as the series of steps needed for us to achieve our plans.

Setting goals is something many individuals and organizations alike attempt doing. Unfortunately, many are unable to do it the right way. In this section of the book, I will take you through the way to go about setting goals the right way.

Anyone can set goals, but only a few are able to do it well. To do this, we will use the acronym, **SMART**[2]. Each of the letters in the acronym has a meaning we will further explore. We will also stick with our example of increasing our numerical strength to ten thousand members, building our own auditorium that would hold thirty thousand members, and establishing fifty branches across the country.

S – Specific: You will realize that we didn't just say, "We want to expand our ministry." That is vague! Expansion could mean many things to many people. That is how many individuals and organizations go about setting goals. They set general goals that they are unable to pursue and achieve. By being specific, we said, "We will INCREASE our NUMERICAL STRENGTH to TEN THOUSAND MEMBERS; BUILD our own AUDITORIUM that can hold THIRTY THOUSAND MEMBERS, and ESTABLISH FIFTY BRANCHES ACROSS THE COUNTRY."

---

[2] Peter Druker, Management by objectives

I used the upper-case letters for emphasis. Every one of what I used the upper-case for is specific. It is not vague. Perhaps, we can even go more specific with our total numerical strength.

Instead of just saying to increase our membership by ten thousand; we can say, we will increase by two thousand men, five thousand women and three thousand children. When we are specific, we are clear on what we want.

As such, we pursue just what we set out to achieve without any confusion. Specificity is a powerful weapon in goal-setting.

M – Measurable: If a goal is measurable; it means it can be tracked over time. We won't wait after twenty years before we come back to assess if we really achieved our long-term plans. That could bring about serious disappointment.

For a goal to be measurable, we need to put certain measurable parameters to it. Not all goals could be measurable in terms of numbers. But somehow, we will definitely need something quantifiable. For example, our long-term plan is to build an auditorium. How do we measure this? After six months, we need to know, have we started scouting for the land that will accommodate the auditorium? If yes, what is next? Have we gone for a land surveyor or building technologist to come assess our site and so on and so forth?

These are definite, measurable steps we will need to take to achieve our plan. With regards to increasing our membership, we will need to keep a register to monitor the regular attendance of members, and a database to keep the details of all members.

How many active members come to church every Sunday, and to every other weekly service?

If the numbers are not impressive, we ask: why? What can we do to get more members? Another way to do this is: we can divide the target number by the total number of years we have.

In our case, we want ten thousand new members in twenty years. This means, we will need at least five hundred new members every year.

We may not hit this target every year, but we need to be sure we are doing something active to help us achieve it and even exceed it.

So after every month, we also expect to have about forty new members. When the goals are broken into such small, measurable numbers, achieving our goals does not look as daunting as having ten thousand new members in twenty years.

A – Achievable: Inasmuch as we want to achieve so much, we have to be sure to set a goal that is attainable, practicable, feasible, or reachable. Is it possible to have ten thousand members after twenty years? Let's say the census figures indicate that our state has just five thousand people, and for the next ten years, the population in our state will increase by a mere ten percent, that means after twenty years, except by some divine intervention, we expect to have a total of six thousand people in the entire state.

Even if we are hopeful to get all these coming to our church, it is impractical because there sure are many other churches and there will probably be more churches within that space of twenty years. So, coming up with a target for numerical increase must be well thought out with consultation with other external factors. That we want to set a goal doesn't mean we set something that excites our ego and yet somehow, is impractical, unattainable, and not feasible.

R – Realistic: A realistic goal sees things from a real and not an ideal point of view. We will have to take a critical look at several other factors, mostly external, to be sure we are being realistic. Under no circumstance should we set a goal that is out of touch with reality.

T – Time-bound: A goal without a timeline is one done in futility. You will realize that we had a definite timeline to our goals. For our long-term plan, we were expected to achieve by twenty years; we set out to achieve our medium-term plans within a period of five to ten years; and from today till five years, we needed to take definite steps to achieve our plans.

When we plan ahead, we are able to FOCUS directly on the strength and skills of the people we lead and help them become their very best. This gives them the opportunity and platform to maximize their potentials.

09

BE A DISCIPLINED LEADER

The absence of discipline can transform any man into a slave

It takes discipline be an effective and impactful leader. Without discipline, a leader will only concede to shame, disgrace and disappointment. Many leaders, mentors, coaches or managers are punching below their weight simply because they lack discipline and, as a result, have suffered a lot of harm just as much as they have put others in harm's way.

Everyone needs discipline to be able to achieve their dreams, goals, and aspirations and being a leader does not exempt you from this principle. Many are in positions of authority but lack the discipline to maintain their roles and to affect lives positively.

Discipline is one of the ladders we all need if we really want to help others get the best in life and to reach their expected end in life. When we are disciplined, we create an atmosphere for success and victory in everything we do with people. That is why anyone called into leadership, mentorship or coaching must ensure they have a disciplined lifestyle in the pursuit of success.

Lack of discipline affects our ability to become what we are meant to be in ministry, leadership, and business, etc. Indiscipline remains a cancer that destroys the cells of growth and progress. When one is undisciplined as a leader, for example, he or she is bound to fail. Disciplined leaders take responsibility for their actions and motives. They don't blame others for their shortcomings. Ill-disciplined leaders find it very comfortable, making excuses for their undisciplined lifestyle rather than owning up and manning up. They develop the habit of blaming others and lack the willingness to initiate a paradigm shift for good. This prevents them from having an open, teachable and ready heart to learn new things in life. It also hinders them from committing to (achieving) a task simply because they have lost focus and attention.

The danger of indiscipline is that it can significantly downsize a leader's ability to influence others positively and cause change within and around his leadership. A disciplined leader is an inspiration and influence to the people he or she leads; but an undisciplined one is a disaster in the making. It was Brian Tracy who said, *"We need men and women who take their responsibilities seriously and are willing to step forward to take command of the situation."*

Most often, some leaders become undisciplined especially when they; become too friendly, compromise, lack personal leadership, lack motivation, and develop bad habits. This can be very detrimental to their leadership.

A disciplined life creates a great sense of accountability and sets you up to deal with personal hurdles or challenges that may limit your success in life. This is why it is prudent that leaders lead disciplined lives both in private and in public.

Leaders ought to develop a spirit of self-discipline, master their self-confidence, self-esteem and inner strength, to produce self-satisfaction. It is sometimes said that, "Leaders with lack of self-discipline often wind up as failures." In view of this, it is orthodox to say that self-discipline is one of the tenets that will enable a leader to remain focused, productive, and successful.

When you look at how an automobile works, its takes into account various parts of the car to be roadworthy. For example, you need the gear box, clutches, brakes, the wheels, head-light, hazard lights and other important parts, to get the car working properly. So, it is vital that you have self-discipline as an integral part of your life to be able to overcome the challenges you are confronted with in your desire to help and empower others.

It takes a lot of discipline to make the right decisions in the face of challenges, trials, and confusion as a leader because the decisions you make as a leader can ease or complicate the following process.

The leader's discipline helps him to lead others in the area of purpose and vision. Great leaders are visionaries. They don't just lead others without vision. Being talented as a coach, mentor or lifestyle professional without discipline to lead with vision is like being on a rollercoaster.

Anyone can stand in a leadership position but not everyone has the discipline to lead by vision. No matter how eloquent a leader is, if you lack the discipline to follow a vision, you will keep vacillating forward, backwards, or sideways without a definite destination in view.

Discipline is paramount for everyone who desires to be successful in life. Discipline is one of the platforms you stand on to reach your success or destiny in life. When your life is disciplined, you create an atmosphere or environment for success and victory in everything you do. That is why you need to ensure that you have a disciplined lifestyle in the pursuit of success.

Lack of discipline affects your ability to become what you are created for in life. It is a cancer to success. Indiscipline prevents an individual from taking responsibility for action to see a dream come true. Such individual is always looking for someone to blame for the outcomes of his or her life. They blame everybody under the sun except themselves.

These individuals find it very comfortable making excuses for their undisciplined lifestyle and not owning up for it; finding it difficult to take responsibility for their actions and make the necessary changes needed for a successful life.

An attitude of indiscipline prevents you from having an open, teachable, and ready heart to learn new things in life and this hinders you from committing or achieving a task for your life.

Most often, some people become undisciplined especially when they get too friendly, compromising, lack personal leadership, lack motivation, and develop bad habits with things and people in their life such as mentors. This can be very detrimental to their destiny or success. A disciplined life establishes a great sense of accountability and sets you up to deal with personal hurdles or challenges that may limit your successful life.

To develop a disciplined life, you need to control the environment you find yourself. Environments are very crucial for the manifestation of your dreams in life and until you take responsibility for the choice of environment or atmosphere, that very atmosphere will affect or prevent you from reaching the mark.

Life is full of challenges and sometimes these challenges tend to distract our focus and purpose for a particular day. However, when you are disciplined enough to remain on track, you will surely get to that place of fulfillment. Imagine that while travelling on a highway (motorway), you come across a number of lights indicating that you reduce your speed limit in the middle of that journey; you do not change your mind on that journey but will surely discipline yourself to continue that journey.

The journey into your destiny will be limited by so many road works, traffic lights and sometimes other drivers pulling in front of, or across you. Without doubt, it will take discipline to remain the good driver you were when you first began the journey without getting upset.

It is very important to avoid the temptation of associating yourself with things that may not enhance the fulfillment of your destiny.

Being disciplined as an individual only enhances and boosts your confidence to pursue your dreams in life. This also creates the platform to accomplish more than you can ever imagine and become more productive by empowering you to develop the right attitude towards frustration, obstacles and negative emotions, which sometimes affect your ability to excel and to reach your most difficult goals without losing steam.

There is no way you can become a person of influence and significance when you lead an unchaste life. Lack of discipline steals your focus in life and even makes you a slave to yourself.

Lack of discipline has the power to make you become a slave to yourself

A disciplined leader brings stability and structure into his leadership. He or she doesn't allow just anyone to operate in his or her leadership without a definitive purpose. Unfortunately, undisciplined leaders accept anything and allow anyone to function within their leadership without accountability. They don't motivate or inspire their followers to conform to rules and regulations and behave accordingly because they themselves are not disciplined enough to lead by example. Such leaders become ineffective in their positions and infect their members with the disease of indiscipline.

In my short experience in leadership, both in ministry and healthcare, I have seen many leaders fail in their roles, causing disappointment and failure to the ministry and/or organization in which they serve because they were not disciplined enough to make sure everyone on the team is properly aligned to the vision and headed in the right (same) direction. Some of these leaders lack proper supervision skills. This prevents them from establishing and enforcing relevant rules. Undisciplined leaders find it difficult to command respect and discipline. Hence, allowing others to do whatever they wish around them without respect of authority.

Leaders who lack discipline find it difficult to communicate effectively

Effective leaders are good with their communication with others because they are disciplined. Such leaders are respected and listened to by everyone in their establishment simply because they are seen to be disciplined. They don't live anyhow and expect others to live otherwise. Disciplined leaders operate with the consciousness that their life is a light and salt for others to live by. This is why they don't live anyhow, but have a principled lifestyle. Such a code of conduct is established on the premise that others will be tempted to live just anyhow and do whatever they wanted without accountability if their leader is found to be loose.

One of the dangers of living an undisciplined life as a leader is that one becomes loose and acts without any sense of decency or propriety. Such leaders destroy confidence and trust.

A leader who loses confidence and trust from the people he leads will find it difficult to lead the people. Disciplined leaders guard their tongue and only speak words that are helpful. They are very careful and mindful about what proceeds from their mouth. Undisciplined leaders don't know when to; hold their mouth, observe or learn. Leaders who are loose with their mouth can't be trusted by anyone in leadership.

Every leader must take due care of what they allow to come off their lips especially when it concerns others within their leadership. Breaching confidentiality as a leader is very hazardous and kills the confidence your teammates have reposed in you. It is the root of self-destruction and sabotage.

As leaders, we are entrusted with people's private and personal information; information which is committed to us in confidence for safekeeping. So, if we are not disciplined enough to keep secrets, we will not be respected and honored.

As leaders, we are expected to keep and maintain the confidentiality of our members regardless of how we feel under the unction or leading of the Holy Spirit. The Holy Spirit is not the author of confusion. Disciplined leaders are very cautious of this fact. As the Bible clearly states, the spirit of the prophet is subject to the prophet.

Leaders in business or ministry should not ignore this. It has a way of making or breaking them. Confidentiality is just as important in ministry as it is when it comes to secular organizations. Breaching members' confidentiality is a mark of indiscipline on the part of the leader. It's therefore very critical that ministers and emerging leaders learn to discipline themselves in this area of confidentiality.

Many lives, marriages, families and destinies have been ruined due to a leader's indiscipline and carelessness with confidential information. The consequences of breaching confidentiality in leadership can be quite devastating. It becomes even more nasty if legal action or redress is pursued by the aggrieved party.

Prophets and clergies should be mindful and cautious of this before they bring their office into disrepute before the law of the land if they are found to be betrayers of trust. Be disciplined to save yourself from unnecessary disgrace and dishonor to your calling. Watch, pray, and avoid this pitfall. Remember, *"He that hath no rule over his own spirit is like a city that is broken down, and without walls"* (Proverbs 25:28).

Assume rule over your own spirit and the fulfillment of your purpose will be a cakewalk.

CONCLUSION

The purpose of man is to influence others positively. We are not meant to dominate people but to help them discover and develop themselves into agents of change. We cannot help others grow into their dreams, aspirations and goals without investing our time, resources and knowledge to help them succeed.

People have so much hidden in them and until we spend quality time and resources on them, their potentials can't be realized and utilized to add value to society.

Bringing out the best in people will help you get on better with people as well as with your personal and professional life. To succeed and win with people, you must respect, value and treat people as individuals and not as groups in order for them to give you their best in whatever they do.

Moreover, trying to help people with their gifts and talents will require patience, skills, and understanding. This is why we need to change some of the methods and approaches we use in helping people and start acting professionally with people to bring out the best in them. No one succeeds in isolation. This is why we all need somebody to help us bring out the best in us so as to fulfil our purpose in life and maximize destiny.

Printed in Great Britain
by Amazon